Saved by a
GHOST

Cover art by *Jane A. Evans*

Saved by a GHOST

True Tales of the Occult

Formerly published under the title *The Perfume of Egypt*

By CHARLES W. LEADBEATER

*This publication made possible
with the assistance of the Kern Foundation*

**The Theosophical Publishing House
Wheaton, Ill. U.S.A.
Madras, India/London, England**

© The Theosophical Publishing House
All rights reserved
First Quest Book edition, 1979, published by the
Theosophical Publishing House, a department of the
Theosophical Society in America. Inquiries for
permission to reproduce all, or portions of this book
should be addressed to Quest Books, 306 West Geneva
Road, Wheaton, Illinois 60187

Library of Congress Cataloging in Publication Data
Leadbeater, Charles Webster, 1847 - 1934
    Saved by a ghost, and other weird stories.

    (Quest books)
    First published under title: The perfume of Egypt.
    CONTENTS: The perfume of Egypt. —The
forsaken temple. —The major's promise. —A test of
courage. —An astral murder. —A triple
warning. (etc.)
    1. Spiritualism. I. Title.
BF1272.L4 1979 133.9 79-9981
ISBN 0-8356-0526-4 pbk.

Printed in the United States of America

FOREWORD

THE stories told in this book happen to be true. Of course I do not for a moment expect the ordinary reader to believe that, and I shall be perfectly satisfied if I succeed in whiling away for him the tedium of a railway journey, or if I can add for him a touch of pleasure to a comfortable evening before the fire or a lazy afternoon on the river.

For the few whose interest in these subjects is not merely superficial, I may add that some of the events related are personal experiences of my own, and that the others are reproduced exactly as they were told to me by persons in whose veracity I have every confidence. In every case, except those of ' Jagannath ' and ' The Baron's Room ', I myself have heard the story directly from the person principally concerned in it, so that there is no place here for the subtle alterations which are inevitably introduced into tales that have passed through many hands. These things happened; and although it may be difficult for one who has made no study of the subject to believe them, those who are familiar with the literature of the occult will readily be able to parallel most of these occurrences.

I have written other and more serious books in which such things as these are scientifically explained; in this volume my only desire is to help my readers to pass pleasantly a few hours of leisure time.

C. W. LEADBEATER

CONTENTS

THE PERFUME OF EGYPT

IT is a curious life, that of a man in chambers, though very pleasant in many ways. Its great charm is its absolute liberty—the entire freedom to go out and come in, or *not* to go out and come in, exactly as one pleases. But it is terribly lonely. Probably most people remember Dickens's tale (founded, I believe, on fact) of a man who was struck by apoplexy when on the point of opening his door, and lay propped up against it for a whole year, until at the expiration of that time it was broken open, and his skeleton fell into the arms of the locksmith. I do not think I am a nervous man, but I confess that during my residence in chambers that story haunted me at times; and indeed, quite apart from such unusual horrors, there is a wide field of uncomfortable possibility in being left so entirely to oneself.

All the most unpleasant things that happen to people, both in fiction and real life, seem to occur when they are alone; and though no doubt the talented American author is right when he ' thanks a merciful heaven that the unendurable extreme of agony happens always to man the unit, and never to man the mass,' one feels that it is probably easier to re-echo his sentiment heartily when one is not the unit in question. On the other hand, when a man in chambers locks his door on a winter night and settles down cosily by the fire for an evening's reading, he has a sense of seclusion and immunity from interruption only to be equalled by that of a man who has sported his oak in a top set in college.

Just so had I [1] settled down—not to reading, however, but to writing—on the evening on which occurred the first of the chain of events that I am about to relate. In fact, I was writing a book—my first book—*On the Present State of the Law on Conveyancing.* I had published several essays on various aspects of the subject, and these had been so well received by high legal authorities, that I was emboldened to present my views in a more ambitious form. It was to this work, then, that I was applying myself with all a young author's zeal on the evening in question; and my reason for mentioning this fact is to show the subject on which my thoughts were fixed with a special intentness—one

[1] The narrator of this remarkable series of incidents (whom I have called Mr. Thomas Keston) is—or rather was—a barrister of considerable repute in London. I have thought it best to leave him to tell his own story in his own words, reserving comments until the end.—C.W.L.

far enough, surely, from suggesting anything like romantic or unusual adventure.

I had just paused, I remember, to consider the exact wording of a peculiarly knotty sentence, when suddenly there came over me that feeling which I suppose all of us have experienced at one time or another—the feeling that I was not alone—that there was some one else in the room. I knew that my door was locked, and that the idea was therefore absurd; yet the impression was so strong that I instinctively half-rose from my chair and glanced hurriedly round. There was nothing visible, however, and with a half-laugh at my foolishness I was turning to my sentence again, when I became conscious of a faint but very peculiar odour in the room. It seemed familiar to me, yet for some few moments I was unable to identify it; then it flashed across my mind where I had met with it before, and my surprise was profound, as will be readily understood when I explain.

I had spent the long vacation of the preceding year in wandering about Egypt, peering into odd nooks and corners, and trying to make myself acquainted with the true life of the country—keeping as far as possible out of the beaten track and away from bands of tourists. While in Cairo I had the good fortune to make the acquaintance of a certain Sheikh (so he was called, though I am

unable to say whether he had any right to the title)
who proved to be a perfect mine of information as
to ancient manners and customs, and the antiquities
of the place generally—as regards relics of the glory
of the mediæval Caliphs, I mean, not the *real* antiquities of the old Egyptian dynasties. My servant
warned me to beware of this man, and said he had
the reputation of being a magician and dealing
extensively with the evil one; however, I always
found him very friendly and obliging, and he certainly pointed out to me many objects of interest
that I should inevitably have missed but for him.

One day, going to call on him at an unusual
hour, I was struck on entering his room by a most
peculiar odour. It was altogether unlike anything
I had ever smelt before—indescribably rich and
sweet—almost oppressively so—and yet its effects
seemed stimulating and exhilarating. I was so
much pleased with it that I pressed the Sheikh
strongly either to give me a little of it or tell me
where I could obtain it; but to my surprise he
refused courteously but firmly to do either. All
he would say was that it was a sacred perfume,
used only in certain incantations; that its manu-
facture was a secret handed down from the remotest
ages and known only to a chosen few; and that not
all the gold in the world would ever buy a single
grain of it.

Naturally this excited my curiosity immensely but he would give me no further information either as to the scent itself or the purpose for which he had been using it. Sitting talking with him for an hour or so, my garments became permeated with its alluring fragrance, and when I returned to my hotel my servant, in brushing my coat, perceived it and started back with horror. Startled out of his usual impassivity and imperturbable courtesy, he asked hurriedly:

" Effendi, where have you been? How comes this devil-scent upon your clothes? "

" What do you mean? " said I. " What is the smell that excites you so strangely? "

" O sir, be careful! " replied my man, almost weeping. " You do not know, you do not believe; you English do not understand the awful power of the old magic of Egypt. I do not know where you have been, but O sir! never go there again, for you have been in terrible danger. Only magicians use this scent, and no magician can make it for himself; it is prepared by devils, and for every phial there must be a human sacrifice, so we call it virgin's blood."

" Nonsense, Mustapha," I said; " you cannot expect me to believe such a tale as that. Cannot you get me some of this mysterious substance? "

"Not for the world," answered Mustapha, with every appearance of mortal dread upon his countenance. "No one can get it—no one, I assure you! and I dare not touch it for my life, even if they could. Effendi, keep away from these things, for your soul's sake."

I laughed at his fear for me, but there could be no doubt that he was in deadly earnest; and it is certainly true that I could find no perfume in the least like that which I remembered so well, though I tried every scent-merchant in Cairo.

When I say that it was this mysterious aroma—faint, but quite unmistakable—that greeted my nostrils in my own chambers in London on that memorable night, it will be seen that I had good reason to be surprised. What could it mean? Was it anyhow possible that the smell could have lingered in some article of clothing? Obviously not, for had it done so I must certainly have discovered the fact in much less time than the fourteen or fifteen months that had elapsed. Then whence could it come? For I was well convinced that nothing in the least like it could be obtained in England. The problem appeared so difficult that when I could no longer perceive the odour I was half inclined to doubt whether after all it might not have been a hallucination; and I turned to my work again, resolved to throw it entirely off my mind.

I worked out the knotty sentence to my satisfaction, and had written perhaps a page more, when quite suddenly and without warning I felt again, more strongly than ever, that unpleasant consciousness of some other presence in the room; but this time, before I could turn to look, I felt—distinctly felt—a soft breath or puff of wind on the back of my neck, and heard a faint sigh. I sprang from my chair with an inarticulate cry, and looked wildly round the room, but there was nothing unusual to be seen—no trace remained of my mysterious visitant. No trace, did I say? Even in the moment that passed while I was regaining my self-possession there stole again upon my astonished sense that strange subtle perfume of ancient eastern magic!

It would be folly to deny that I was seriously startled. I rushed to the door and tried it—shook it vigorously; but it was locked, exactly as I had left it. I turned in the bedroom; there was no one there. I then searched both the rooms thoroughly looking under bed, sofas, and tables, and opening every cupboard or box large enough to hold even a cat; still there was nothing. I was completely puzzled. I sat down and tried to think the matter out, but the more I thought the less could I see my way to any rational solution of these occurrences.

At length I decided to shake off their influence for the time, and postpone all consideration of them until the morning. I tried to resume my work, but I was out of tune for writing—my mind had been too much disturbed. The haunting consciousness of another presence would not leave me; that soft sad sigh seemed yet sounding in my ears, and its unutterable sorrow provoked a feeling of sympathetic depression. After a few unavailing efforts I gave up the attempt to write, threw myself into an armchair by the fire, and began to read instead.

Though simple enough, I believe, in most of my habits, I am rather a Sybarite about my reading; for that purpose I always use the most comfortable armchair that money can procure, with that most blessed of inventions, the 'Literary Machine', to hold my book at exactly the right angle, shade the light from my face and concentrate it on the page, and give me a desk always ready to my hand if I wish to make notes.

In this luxurious manner, then, I settled myself down on this occasion, choosing as my book Montaigne's *Essays*, in the hope that their cleverness and marvellous flexibility of style might supply just the mental tonic that I felt I needed. Ignore them as I might, however, I had still as I read two under-currents of consciousness—one of that ever-haunting presence, and the other of occasional faint waftings of the perfume of Egypt.

I suppose I had been reading for about half an hour when a stronger whiff than ever greeted my nostrils, and at the same time a slight rustle caused me to raise my eyes from my book. Judge of my astonishment when I saw, not five yards from me, seated at the table from which I had so lately risen, and apparently engaged in writing, the figure of a man! Even as I looked at him the pen fell from his hand, he rose from the chair, threw upon me a glance which seemed to express bitter disappointment and heart-rending appeal, and— vanished!

Too much stupefied even to rise, I sat staring at the spot where he had stood, and rubbed my eyes mechanically, as though to clear away the last relics of some horrible dream. Great as the shock had been, I was surprised to find, as soon as I was able to analyze my sensations, that they were distinctly those of relief; and it was some minutes before I could comprehend this. At last it flashed across me that the haunting sense of an unseen presence was gone, and then for the first time I realized how terrible its oppression had been. Even that strange magical odour was rapidly fading away, and in spite of the startling sight I had just seen, I had a sense of freedom such as a man feels when he steps out of some dark dungeon into the full bright sunlight.

2

Perhaps it was this feeling more than anything else that served to convince me that what I had seen was no delusion—that there had really been a presence in the room all the time which had at last succeeded in manifesting itself, and now was gone. I forced myself to sit still and recall carefully all that I had seen—even to note it down on the paper which lay before me on the desk of my literary machine.

First, as to the personal appearance of my ghostly visitor, if such he were. His figure was tall and commanding, his face expressing great power and determination, but showing also traces of a reckless passion and possible latent brutality that certainly gave on the whole the impression of a man rather to be feared and avoided than loved. I noticed more particularly the firm setting of his lips, because running down from the under one there was a curious white scar, which this action caused to stand out conspicuously; and then I recollected how this expression had broken and changed to one in which anger, despair, and appeal for help were strangely mingled with a certain dark pride that seemed to say:

"I have done all I could; I have played my last card and it has failed; I have never stooped to ask help from mortal man before, but I ask it from you now."

A good deal, you will say, to make out of a single glance; but still that was exactly what it seemed to me to express; and, sinister though his appearance was, I mentally resolved that his appeal should not have been made in vain, if I could in any way discover who he was or what he wanted. I had never believed in ghosts before; I was not even quite sure that I did now; but clearly a fellow-creature in suffering was a brother to be helped, whether in the body or out of the body. With such thoughts as these all trace of fear vanished, and I honestly believe that if the spirit had reappeared I should have asked him to sit down and state his case as coolly as I should have met any other client.

I carefully noted down all the events of the evening, appended the hour and date, and affixed my signature; and then, happening to look up, my eye was caught by two or three papers lying on the floor. I had seen the wide sleeve of the long dark gown that the spectre wore sweep them down as he rose, and this for the first time reminded me that he had appeared to be writing at the table, and consequently might possibly have left there some clue to the mystery. At once I went and examined it; but everything was as I had left it, except that my pen lay where I had seen it fall from his hand. I picked up the papers from the floor, and then— my heart gave a great bound, for I saw among them a curious torn fragment which had certainly not been on my table before.

The eagerness with which I seized upon it may be imagined. It was a little oblong slip about five inches by three, apparently part either of a longer slip or a small book, for its edge at one end was extremely jagged, suggesting that considerable force had been required to tear it off; and indeed the paper was so thick and parchment-like that I could not wonder at it. The curious thing was that while the paper was much discoloured—water-stained and yellow with age—the jagged edge was white and fresh, looking as though it had been but just torn off. One side of the paper was entirely blank—or at least, if there ever had been any writing upon it, it had disappeared through the influence of time and damp; on the other were some blurred and indistinct characters, so faded as to be scarcely distinguishable, and, in a bold handwriting in fresh black ink the two letters 'Ra'.

Since the ink with which these letters were written corresponded exactly with that which I was in the habit of using, I could hardly doubt that they had been written at my table, and were the commencement of some explanation that the spectre had wished, but for some reason found himself unable, to make. Why he should have taken the trouble to bring his own paper with him

I could not understand, but I inferred that probably some mystery was hidden beneath those undecipherable yellow marks, so I turned all my attention to them. After patient and long-continued effort, however, I was unable to make anything like sense out of them, and resolved to wait for daylight.

Contrary to my expectations, I did *not* dream of my ghostly visitor that night, though I lay awake for some time thinking of him. In the morning I borrowed a magnifying glass from a friend, and resumed my examination. I found that there were two lines of writing, apparently in some foreign language, and then a curious mark, not unlike a monogram of some kind, standing as if in the place of a signature. But with all my efforts I could neither distinguish the letters of the monogram nor discover the language of the two lines of writing. As far as I could make it out it read thus:

Qomm uia daousa sita eo uia uiese quoam.

Some of these words had rather a Latin look; and I reflected that if the memorandum were as old as it appeared to be, Latin was a very likely language for it; but then I could make out nothing like a coherent sentence, so I was as far off from a solution as ever. I hardly knew what steps to take next. I shrank so much from speaking of the events of that evening that I could not bring myself to show the slip to any one else, lest it should lead to enquiries as to how it came into my possession; I so put it away carefully in my pocket-book, and for the time being my investigations seemed at a standstill.

I had not gained any fresh light on the subject, nor come to any definite conclusion about it, by the time the second incident of my story occurred, about a fortnight later. Again I was sitting at my writing-table early in the evening—engaged this time not upon my book but in the less congenial pursuit of answering letters. I dislike letter-writing, and am always apt to let my correspondence accumulate until the arrears assume formidable proportions, and insist on attention; and then I devote a day or two of purgatory to it, and clear them up. This was one of these occasions, further accentuated by the fact that I had to decide which of three Christmas invitations I would accept.

It had been my custom for years always to spend Christmas when in England with my brother and his family, but this year his wife's health compelled them to winter abroad. I am conservative—absurdly so, I fear—about small things like this, and I felt that I should not really enjoy my Christmas at any house but his, so I cared little to choose in the matter. Here, however, were the three invitations; it was already the fourteenth of December, and I had not yet made up my mind. I was still debating the subject when I was disturbed by a loud knock at my door. On opening it I was confronted by a handsome sunburnt young fellow, whom at first I could not recognize; but when he called out in cheery tones:

"Why, Keston, old fellow, I believe you've forgotten me!"

I knew him at once as my old school-fellow Jack Fernleigh. He had been my fag at Eton, and I had found him such a jolly, good-hearted little fellow that our 'official' relation had glided into a firm friendship—a very rare occurrence; and though he was so far junior to me at Oxford that we were together there only a few months, still our acquaintance was kept up, and I had corresponded with him in a desultory sort of way ever since. I knew, consequently, that some years ago he had had some difference with his uncle (his only living relation) and had gone off to the West Indies to seek his fortune; and though our letters had been few and far between, I knew in a general way that he was doing very well there, so it was with no small surprise that I saw him standing at the door of my chambers in London.

I gave him a hearty welcome, set him down by the fire, and then asked him to explain his presence in England. He told me that his uncle had died suddenly, leaving no will, and that the lawyers had telegraphed the news to him. He had at once thrown up his position and started for England by the next steamer. Arriving in London too late to see his lawyers that day, and having after his long absence no other friends there, he had come, as he expressed it, to see whether I had forgotten my old fag.

"And right glad I am that you did, my boy," said I; "where is your luggage? We must send to the hotel for it, for I shall make you up a bed here for to-night.

He made a feeble protest, which I at once over-ruled; a messenger was found and despatched to the hotel, and we settled down for a talk about old times which lasted far into the night. The next morning he went betimes to call upon his lawyers, and in the afternoon started for Fernleigh Hall (now his property), but not before we had decided that I should run down and spend Christmas there with him instead of accepting any of my three previous invitations.

"I expect to find everything in a terrible state," he said; "but in a week's time I shall be able to get things a little to rights, and if you will turn up on the twenty-third I will promise you at least a bed to sleep in, and you will be doing a most charitable action in preventing my first Christmas in England for many a year from being a lonely one."

So we settled it, and consequently at four o'clock on the afternoon of the twenty-third I was shaking hands again with Jack on the platform of the little country station a few miles from Fernleigh. The short day had already drawn to a close by the time we reached the house, so I could get only a general idea of its outside appearance. It was a large Elizabethan mansion, but evidently not in very good repair; however, the rooms into which we were ushered were bright and cheerful enough. We had a snug little dinner, and after it Jack proposed to show me over the house. Accordingly, preceded by a solemn old butler with a lamp, we wandered through interminable mazes of rambling passages, across great desolate halls, and in and out of dozens of tapestried and panelled bedrooms—some of them with walls of enormous thickness, suggestive of all sorts of trap-doors and secret outlets—till my brain became absolutely confused, and I felt as though, if my companions had abandoned me, I might have spent days in trying to find my way out of the labyrinth.

" You could accommodate an army here, Jack! ' said I.

"Yes," he replied, "and in the good old days Fernleigh was known all over the country for its open hospitality; but now, as you see, the rooms are bare and almost unfurnished."

"You'll soon change all that when you bring home a nice little wife", I said; "the place only wants a lady to take care of it."

"No hope of it, my dear fellow, I'm sorry to say", replied Jack; "there is not enough money for that."

I knew how in our school-days he had worshipped with all a boy's devotion lovely Lilian Featherstone, the daughter of the rector of the parish, and I had heard from him at college that on his part at least their childish intimacy had ripened into something deeper; so I asked after her now, and soon discovered that his sojourn in the tropics had worked no change in his feelings in this respect, that he had already contrived to meet her and her father out riding since his return, and that he had good reason to hope from her blush of pleasure on seeing him that he had not been forgotten in his absence. But alas! her father had only his living to depend on, and Jack's uncle (a selfish profligate) had not only let everything go to ruin, but had also so encumbered the estate that, by the time all was paid off and it was entirely free, there was but little money left—barely sufficient to support Jack himself, and certainly not enough to marry upon.

"So there is no hope of Lilian yet, you see," he concluded; "but I am young and strong; I can work, and I think she will wait for me. You shall see her on Thursday, for I have promised that we will dine with them then; they would have insisted on having me on Christmas day, but that I told them I had an old school-fellow coming down."

Just then we reached the door of the picture-gallery, and the old butler, having thrown it open, was proceeding to usher us in, but I said:

"No Jack, let us leave this until tomorrow; we cannot see pictures well by this light. Let us go back to the fire, and you shall tell me that old legend of your family that was so much talked about at college; I never heard more than the merest fragments of it."

"There is nothing worth calling a legend", said Jack, as we settled down in the cosy little room he called his study; "nor is it very old, for it refers only to the latter part of the eighteenth century. The interest of the story, such as it is, centres round Sir Ralph Fernleigh, the last baronet, who seems by all accounts to have been a somewhat questionable character. He is said to have been a strange, reserved man—a man of strong passions, iron will, and indomitable pride; he spent much of his time abroad, and was reported to have acquired enormous wealth by means that would not bear too close examination. He was commonly known as 'wicked Sir Ralph', and the more superstitious of his neighbours firmly believed that he had studied the black art during his long absences in the East. Others hinted that he was owner of a privateer, and that in those troubled times it was easy for a reckless man to commit acts of piracy with impunity.

"He was credited with a great knowledge of jewels, and was reported to possess one of the most splendid private collections of them in the world; but as none were found by his successor, I conclude that unless they were stolen the story was a myth, like that which represented him as having bars of gold and silver stacked up in his cellars. It seems certain that he was really tolerably ricn, and that during his later years, which he spent here, he lived a remarkably retired life. He discharged all servants but a confidential man of his own, an Italian who had accompanied him in his wanderings; and these two lived a sort of hermit-life here all by themselves, holding no intercourse with the outer world. The universal report was that, though he had stored up great hoards of ill-gotten wealth, Sir Ralph lived like a miser. The few people who had seen him whispered darkly of a haunted look always to be seen on his proud face, and talked beneath their breath of some terrible secret crime; but I do not know that anything was ever really proved against him.

"One morning, however, he mysteriously disappeared; at least such was the story of the Italian servant, who came one day to the village asking in a frightened way in his broken English whether any one had seen his master. He said that, two days before, Sir Ralph had in the evening ordered his horse to be saddled early on the following morning, as he was going on a short journey alone; but when the morning came, though the horse was ready, *he* was not. He did not answer to his servant's calls, and though the latter searched through every room in the great old house, not a trace of his master could he find. His bed, he said, had not been slept in that night, and the only theory he could offer was that he had been carried away by the demons he used to raise. The villagers suspected foul play, and there was a talk of arresting the servant—which, coming to the latter's ears, seems to have alarmed him so much (in his ignorance of the customs of the country) that *he* also mysteriously disappeared that night, and was never seen again.

"Two days afterwards an exploring party was formed by the more adventurous of the villagers. They went all over the house and grounds, examined every nook and corner, and shouted themselves hoarse; 'but there was no voice, neither any that answered', and from that day to this no sign either of master or man has ever revisited the light of the sun. Since the explorers could find none of the rumoured hoards of money either, it was an accepted article of faith among them that 'that there furriner' had murdered his master, hidden his body, and carried off the treasure, and of course a story presently arose that Sir Ralph's ghost had been seen about the place.

"They whispered that his room might be known from all the rest in this dark old house by a peculiar atmosphere of its own, caused by the constant haunting of the unquiet spirit of the owner; but this soon became a mere tradition, and now no one knows even in what part of the house his room was, nor have I ever heard of the ghost's appearance in my uncle's time, though I know he half-believed in it and never liked to speak of it. After Sir Ralph's disappearance the place was unoccupied and neglected for some years, till at last a distant cousin put in a claim to it, got it allowed by the lawyers, and took possession. He found, it is said, but a small balance after all to Sir Ralph's credit at his bankers'; but he had money of his own, apparently, for he proceeded to refit and rearrange the old place, and soon had it in respectable order. From him it descended to my uncle, who has let everything run to seed again, as you see."

" That is a very interesting family legend after all, Jack ", said I, " though perhaps rather lacking in romantic completeness. But have you no relics of this mysterious Sir Ralph? "

" There is his portrait in the picture-gallery along with the rest; there are some queer old books of his in the library, and one or two articles of furniture that are reported to have been his; but there is nothing to add to the romance of the story, I am afraid."

Little he thought, as he uttered those words just as we were separating for the night, what the real romance of that story was, or how soon we were to discover it!

My bedroom was a huge panelled chamber with walls of prodigious thickness, and with some very beautiful old carving about it. A border of roses and lilies that ran round the panels especially attracted my attention as one of the finest examples of that style of work that I had ever seen. There is always, I think, something uncanny about great Elizabethan bedrooms and huge four-post bedsteads, and I suppose my late ghostly experience had rendered me specially alive to such influences; so, though the roaring fire which Jack's hospitable care had provided for me threw a cheery light into every corner, I found myself thinking as I lay down in bed:

"What if this should turn out to be Sir Ralph's forgotten chamber, and he should come and disturb my rest, as that other visitor came to me in town!"

This idea returned to me again and again, until I really began to fancy that I could distinguish the peculiar atmosphere of which Jack had spoken—a sort of subtle influence that was gradually taking possession of me. This I felt would never do, if I was to have a comfortable night, so I roused myself from this unhealthy train of thought and resolutely put it away from me; but do what I would, I could not entirely shake off ghostly associations, for (recalled I suppose by my surroundings) every detail of the strange occurrence at my chambers passed before my mind over and over again with startling distinctness and fidelity.

Eventually I fell into a troubled sleep, in which my late mysterious visitor and the idea I had formed of Sir Ralph Fernleigh seemed to chase each other through my brain, till at last all these confused visions culminated in one peculiarly vivid dream. I seemed to myself to be lying in bed (just as I really was), with the fire burnt down to a deep red glow, when suddenly there appeared before me the same figure that I had seen in my chambers, habited in the same loose black robe; but now it held in its left hand a small book—evidently that to which the slip in my possession had belonged, for I could see the very place from which the missing leaf had been torn—and with the forefinger of the right hand the spectre was pointing to the last page of the book, while it looked eagerly in my face.

I sprang up and approached the figure; it retreated before me until it reached one of the pannelled walls, through which it seemed to vanish, still pointing to the page of its book, and with that imploring gaze still on its face. I woke with a start, and found myself standing close to the wall at the spot where the figure had seemed to disappear, with the dull red glow of the fire reflected from the carving, just as I had seen it in my dream, and my nostrils filled once more with that strange sweet Oriental perfume! Then in a moment a revelation dawned upon my mind. There was a peculiarity in the atmosphere of the room—I had been quite right in fancying so; and that peculiarity, which I could not recognize before, consisted in the faintest possible permanent suggestion of that magical odour—so faint that I had not been able to identify it until this stronger rush of the scent made it clear.

Was it a dream, I asked myself; or had I really seen my mysterious visitor once more? I could not tell, but at any rate the smell in the room was an

3

undoubted fact. I went and tried the door, but, as I expected, found it as I left it—fast locked. I stirred up my fire into a bright blaze, threw fresh coals on it, and went to bed again—this time to sleep soundly and refreshingly till I was awakened in the morning by the servant bringing hot water.

Reviewing my last night's adventure in the sober light of day, I was disposed to think that something of it at least might be due to overheated imagination, though I still fancied I could detect that faint peculiarity of atmosphere. I decided to say nothing to Fernleigh, since to speak of it would involve describing the apparition in my chambers, which I shrank from discussing with any one; so when Jack asked me how I had slept, I replied:

"Very well indeed towards morning, though a little restless in the earlier part of the night."

After breakfast we walked about the park, which was very extensive, and studied the stately old house from different points of view. I was much struck with the great beauty of its situation and surroundings; and, though there were sad traces of neglect everywhere, I saw that the expenditure of what was comparatively but a small amount of money for so large a place would make it fully worthy to rank with any mansion and estate of its size in the kingdom. I enthusiastically pointed out the various possibilities to Jack, but he, poor fellow, sorrowfully remarked that the sum required to make the improvements, though no doubt comparatively small, was absolutely pretty large, and far beyond his present means.

After some hours' ramble we returned to the house, and Jack proposed that we should look over the picture-gallery and some other rooms that we had not seen on the previous night. We took the gallery first, and Jack told me that it had once contained many almost priceless gems of the old Flemish and Italian masters; but his dissolute uncle had sold most of them, often at merely nominal prices, to raise money for his riotous life in town, so that what were left were, generally speaking, comparatively valueless. There was the usual collection of ancestral portraits—some life-like and carefully executed, others mere daubs; and we were passing them over with scant interest, when my eye was caught by one which instantly riveted my attention and sent a cold thrill down my spine, bright midday though it was; for there, out of the canvas, looked the very face I had seen so vividly in my dream last night—the face of the mysterious visitant at my chambers in London!

The commanding look of iron will and dauntless courage was there, and the same indefinable air of latent passion and cruelty; there too, though tenderly treated by the artist and made less prominent than it was in reality, was the curious white scar running down from the lower lip. Except that he was here dressed in rich court costume instead of the plain black robe, nothing but the pleading look of appeal was wanting to make the resemblance exact. I suppose something of the emotion I felt showed itself in my face, for Jack seized me by the arm, crying:

"Bless me, Tom, what is the matter? Are you ill? Why are you glaring at the portrait of Sir Ralph in that awful manner?"

"Sir Ralph? Yes, the wicked Sir Ralph. I know him. He came into my room last night. I've seen him twice."

Muttering these disjointed sentences, I staggered to an ottoman and tried to collect my scattered senses. For the whole truth had flashed upon me, and it was almost too much for me. Of course it has occurred to the intelligent reader long ago, but until this moment absolutely no suspicion had ever crossed my mind that Sir Ralph and my spectral visitor in London were identical; now I saw it all. The word commencing with 'Ra' that he had tried so hard to write was his own name; he had somehow (heaven alone knows how) foreseen that I should visit Fernleigh, and so had tried to make an impression on my mind—introduce himself to me, as it were—beforehand. I was now obliged to tell

Jack the whole story, and was relieved to find that instead of laughing at me, as I more than half expected, he was deeply interested.

" I never believed in a ghost before," he said, " but here there seems no room for doubt. A perfect stranger shows himself to you in London, you recognize his portrait at once on sight down here at Fernleigh, and he turns out to be the very man whom tradition points out as haunting this place! The chain of evidence is perfect."

" But why should he have come to *me*? " I said. " I know nothing about ghosts and their ways; I am not even what these spiritualists call mediumistic. Would it not have been much more straightforward to appeal to you direct? Why should *I* be singled out for such a visitation? "

" Impossible to say ", replied Jack; " I suppose he liked your looks; but what could he have wanted? We are no nearer discovering that than we were before. Where is that scrap of paper? For it strikes me that the solution of its mystery will yield the answer to our riddle."

I pulled out my pocket-book and handed the slip to Jack.

" Ha! " he exclaimed, the moment he glanced at it, " this is certainly Sir Ralph's monogram; I know it well, for I have seen it in several of the books in the library."

We at once adjourned to the library and compared the writing in some of Sir Ralph's books with that on the slip; the resemblance was perfect, though the writing on the slip seemed more carefully done, as though with a special effort to make every letter legible: while in the monogram (a very complicated one) every line and stroke were exactly similar. With Jack's guidance I was able to make out of it the initials ' R.F.', but I should certainly never have discovered them without assistance. We now concentrated our attention on the two lines of writing.

Jack took a powerful glass from a drawer and scrutinized them long and carefully.

" Your reading of the letters seems quite correct ", he said at length; " but what language can this possibly be? It is not Spanish, Portuguese, nor Italian, I know; and you, who are acquainted with several Oriental dialects, do not recognize it either. I don't believe it is a language at all, Tom; it looks much more like a cryptograph."

" Scarcely, I think," I remarked; " you know, in a cryptograph one always gets utterly impossible combinations of consonants which betray its nature at once."

" Not invariably ", replied Jack; " that depends upon the system on which it is constructed. I happen, though only by way of pastime, to have made this subject a rather special study, and I do not think there are many cryptographs which I could not, with sufficient time and patience, manage to make out."

"Then, Jack, if you think this may be one, by all means proceed to exercise your talents upon it at once."

Jack set to work, and I must say I was really amazed at the ingenuity he displayed, and the facility with which he seized upon and followed up the most seemingly insignificant clues. I need give no particulars of his processes; thanks to Edgar Allen Poe, everybody in these days knows how a cryptograph is solved. Suffice it to say that this, though really extremely simple, gave a good deal of trouble and led us off on a false scent, in consequence of the fact that a double system is employed in its construction. The rule is to substitute for every consonant the letter succeeding it in the alphabet, but for every vowel—not the letter, but— the *vowel* next *preceding* it in the alphabet. By a reversal of this process the reader will easily discover that its signification is as follows:

Pull the centre rose in the third panel.

Our excitement may be imagined when this was deciphered. I knew at once to what it referred, for I remembered the carved border of roses and lilies round the panels in my bedroom of last night. The butler came in to announce luncheon, but we cared little for that; we rushed upstairs like a couple of school-boys and dashed into the panelled room.

"The third panel from which end?" asked Jack.

But I had not the slightest doubt; I remembered that the spectre had vanished through the wall on the left of the fireplace, so I walked up to that spot without hesitation, put my hand on the third panel from the corner, and said:

"This is it."

So large was the panel, however, that the centre rose was above our reach, and it was necessary to drag a table underneath it to stand upon. Jack sprang upon it and gave an energetic pull at the centre rose, but no result followed.

"Get down again," I said; "let us try the other side of the panel."

We moved the table, and Jack tried again, and this time with success. A small piece of the border had been cut out and hinged at the top, and the pull upon the rose lifted this and disclosed a cavity about six inches each way, in which was a large knob—evidently a handle. For some time this resisted our efforts, the machinery attached being probably rusty; but eventually we succeeded in turning it, and the whole huge panel swung into the room like a door, showing behind it a dark arched recess with steps leading downward, up which came, stronger than ever, that strange sweet smell of the perfume of Egypt which had haunted my thoughts so long. Jack was springing in, but I held him back.

"Stay, my dear fellow," I said; "curb your impatience. That place probably has not been opened for a very long time, and you must first let the fresh air penetrate it; you don't know what noxious gases may have accumulated down in that dreadful hole. Besides, we must first lock the door of the bedroom, that we may not be interrupted in our investigation."

Finally I persuaded him to wait five minutes, though in our excited condition it was a hard thing to do. Meantime we could not but admire the enormous strength of the walls, and the care that had been taken to make the moving panel safe by a massive backing of oak that prevented it from giving anything like a hollow sound if accidentally struck, and indeed made it as capable of resisting any conceivable blow as any other portion of the wall. When we noticed, too, the immense size and strength of the lock it had to move, we no longer wondered at the trouble it had cost us to turn the handle.

When the five minutes had expired we lighted a couple of candles that stood on the mantelpiece, and with mingled feelings of awe and pleasure entered the secret passage. The stairs turned abruptly to the left, and descended in the thickness of the wall. My fears as to want of ventilation seemed groundless, for there was quite a strong draught, proving that there must be an opening of some kind in the passage.

At the bottom of the steps we found ourselves in a long narrow vault or chamber, scarcely six feet in width, but perhaps thirty in length, and certainly fourteen or fifteen in height. Floor and walls were alike stone, and at the extreme and near the roof, quite out of reach, was a small slit such as those made of old for the convenience of archers, through which came a certain amount of light, and the current of air that we had noticed. On the floor at the further end were two large chests—the only furniture of this dungeon—and on one of them lay a black heap that by the flickering light of our candles looked horribly like a shrouded corpse.

"What can that be?" said I, shrinking back instinctively; but Jack pushed on to the end of the vault, and then dropped his candle with a smothered cry and came back towards me with a very white face.

"It is a dead body," he said in a horror-stricken whisper; "it must be Sir Ralph."

"Then," said I in the same tone, "he must have been shut in here somehow and starved to death."

"Good heavens!" cried Jack; and he rushed past me and up the stairs at full speed. At first I thought he had lost his nerve and deserted me, but in a few moments he was back again, though still pale with emotion.

"Just think, Tom," he said; "suppose a gust of wind had shut that door, the very same thing might have happened to us! No one knows of the existence of this place, so they would never think of looking here for us; and with such a massive door as that, it would be hopeless to dream of forcing our way out or making ourselves heard. Now I have fixed it open, and we are safe."

"Horrible as it is, I suppose we must examine this thing", I said.

We approached it, Jack picking up and relighting his candle. The sight that met our eyes was truly an awful one, for there, stretched on the top of one of the chests, and wrapped in a loose black robe with wide sleeves, lay a skeleton, with its grinning face turned upwards and its arm thrown carelessly over the side as if in ghastly imitation of sleep. Beside it on the floor lay a curiously shaped wide-mouthed bottle, and on the other chest—and I shuddered afresh as I recognized it—the very memorandum-book that the spectre had carried in my dream! I took it up, and we at once proceed to examine it. It opened at the place where leaf had been newly torn out, but I turned hastily to those last pages at which the figure had pointed so earnestly, and there read the following words:

I, Ralph Fernleigh, Bart., do here indite these my last dying words. By the judgment of God or by some foul treachery I am fast shut up in this mine own secret place, from which is no escape. Here I have lain three days and three nights, and forasmuch as I see naught before me but to die by hunger, I am now resolved to put an end to this my so miserable existence by eating of those poisonous gums, whereof I have happily some store. But first will I confess the deadly sin that lieth upon my soul, and will lay solemn charge upon him who shall here find my body and shall read this my writing.[1]

*   *   *   *   *

And if he who reads these my words shall fail to make such restitution as I have charged upon him, or shall reveal ever to mortal man this my deadly sin that I have here confessed, then shall my solemn curse rest upon him for ever, and my spirit shall dog him even to his grave. But if he shall do faithfully this my behest, then do I hereby freely give and bequeath to him such wealth as he will here find, hoping that he may use it to better purpose than I have done. And so may God have mercy on my soul.

RALPH FERNLEIGH

---

[1] The document itself explains why my friend was compelled to omit some part of it.—C.W.L.

How deeply we were affected by thus, in the very presence of his mortal remains, reading this strange message from the dead, may easily be imagined. Jack had picked up the wide-mouthed bottle, at the bottom of which still remained some dark-coloured resinous matter—evidently the 'poisonous gums' of the writing; but on hearing of its terrible association he dashed it on the floor in horror, and it was broken into a thousand pieces. Nor could I censure him for the act, though I knew that it contained the perfume of Egypt that I had so long desired. (I may here mention that I afterwards recovered a few grains and subjected it to analysis; it proved to be the Persian *lôbhán*, but mixed with belladonna, Indian hemp, and some other vegetable ingredients whose exact nature I was unable to determine.)

Our next duty was the examination of the chests; but to perform this it was necessary first to remove the skeleton, and that we shrank from touching or even looking at. Still it had to be done, so we fetched a sheet from the bedroom, laid the ghastly relic reverently upon that, and so lifted it from the bed where it had laid so long. Then, not without a feeling of excitement, we opened the chests—a work of no difficulty, for the key that was in the lock of one fitted that of the other as well. The first was closely packed with bags and smaller boxes, the former of which, to our astonishment, we found to contain chiefly gold and silver coin of various countries; while the latter proved the truth of at least one of the popular rumours about Sir Ralph, for arranged carefully in them was a collection of gems, cut and uncut, some of which even our inexperienced eyes could tell to be almost priceless.

"Jack, my boy," said I, grasping his hand (for not even the presence of the skeleton could altogether restrain my joy), "you shall soon wed your Lilian now! Even after carrying out Sir Ralph's wishes you will still be a rich man."

"Yes, Tom," answered he; "but remember, half of this is yours; without you I should never have known of its existence.

"No, no," replied I; "not a penny will I touch; I have enough and to spare, and besides it is all yours by right, for you are Sir Ralph's heir."

But he insisted, and at last to pacify him I had to consent to accept one or two of the larger jewels as mementoes. The other chest contained a great quantity of family plate, some of it very rich and massive, and half a dozen small bars of gold, probably the basis of the wild myth that I mentioned before.

By the time our investigations were finished evening had come on; and, as may be supposed we sat down to dinner with an appetite, and after it was over sat talking and planning far into the night. Very happily, though very quietly, we spent our Christmas day, and on the Thursday we dined at the rectory as arranged. Certainly Jack had not exaggerated the charms of his fair Lilian, and when in the course of the evening I saw them come out of the conservatory together, both looking greatly discomposed but deliciously happy, I knew that I might safely offer the dear fellow my congratulations.

I have little more to tell. The dying charge of Sir Ralph was scrupulously obeyed. Jack and I paid a visit to a somewhat out-of-the-way part of the Continent, and spent some time in searching through old records and unravelling forgotten genealogies; but after much toil we met with gratifying success, and at long last atonement was made—so far as in such cases atonement ever can be made—for the sin of the previous century, and the traditional hatred which certain families bore to the memory of a magic-working English lord was changed into a vivid and surprised gratitude. All was done that could be done; indeed, Jack was most lavishly generous, and we have every reason to hope that Sir Ralph was satisfied. At any rate, he has never since shown himself, either to praise or to blame us; so we trust that his long-tormented soul is at peace.

Three months later, in the sweet early spring-time, I went down to Fernleigh again to act as

' best man ' at a wedding and as we passed down the churchyard the happy bridegroom silently pointed out to me a white marble cross bearing simply the words:

SIR RALPH FERNLEIGH, BART.

1795.

Though not myself an eye-witness of the events of this story, I received them on unimpeachable testimony; in fact I may say that I had evidence for them such as would have satisfied any ordinary jury. With the narrator I had the pleasure of an intimate acquaintance of some years' duration. His friend Mr. Fernleigh I have seen only once, when he was in town for a few days; but on that occasion he fully and circumstantially corroborated Mr. Keston's account of these strange events and gave me a warm and hearty invitation to come down and spend a fortnight at the Hall, so as to examine the theatre of their occurrence at my leisure; and further, as my engagements compelled me regretfully to forego the pleasure of this interesting visit, he was good enough to take the trouble to send up to Mr. Keston (for my inspection) the curious old memorandum-book and the torn leaf containing the cryptograph which occupies so prominent a place in the narrative.

Whether or not my friend is right in describing himself as not mediumistic in the ordinary sense of the word is uncertain. There are certain peculiarities in his character which may help to explain what seems to have puzzled him so much—the reason why Sir Ralph should have selected *him* to receive his communication. He is pre-eminently a man of deep feeling, of intense and ready sympathy, as indeed may be seen from the narrative; a man who reminds one of those lines of Béranger:

Son cœur est un luth suspendu;
Sitot qu'on le touche il resonne.

Probably this capability of sympathy attracted Sir Ralph as a channel through which his purpose could be carried out.

The story seems to me to differ from other accounts of the visitations of ' earth-bound souls ' only (1) in the appearance of the wraith in the first place at a distance from the scene of death and to a person in no way specially connected with it, and (2) in the foreknowledge which the dead man seems to have possessed of that person's visit to his former home—not only before the invitation was given, but even before the *idea* of the invitation (which, as far as we can see, was quite accidental) could possibly have existed in the mind of either host or guest. This latter is the

4

point which seems to me most difficult to explain, since such foreknowledge would appear to indicate a power of prevision much more considerable than that with which men in such a condition can usually be credited. It is probable that Sir Ralph's attention was attracted to Mr. Keston in consequence of the bond of friendship existing between him and Mr. John Fernleigh, and that, finding him to be sufficiently impressionable to receive his communication, he endeavoured to deliver his message to him in his chambers; but, failing in that attempt, he influenced Mr. Fernleigh (as he might easily do) to invite him into his own peculiar domain, where his power was naturally greater. The fact that the strange, rare and magical perfume of Egypt was known to both men must be regarded simply as a coincidence, though a dramatic one.

THE FORSAKEN TEMPLE

MANY years ago I was living in a little village seven or eight miles from London—a quiet, straggling, old-fashioned place that might from its appearance have been a hundred miles at least from any of the busy centres of commerce. *Now* it is a village no longer, for the giant city, in its steady, resistless expansion, has absorbed it into itself; the old coach-road, once an avenue of great elm-trees as fine as any in the kingdom, is now flanked by trim suburban villas; a new railway station has been opened, and cheap workmen's tickets are issued; and the dear old picturesque, draughty, wooden cottages have been pulled down to make way for model artisans' dwellings. Well, I suppose it is the march of improvement—the advance of civilization; and yet, perhaps, an old inhabitant may be excused for doubting whether the people were not healthier and happier in the quiet village days.

I had not been long in the place before I made the acquaintance of the clergyman of the district, and offered him such assistance as lay in my power in his parish work. This he was kind enough to accept, and finding that I was fond of children, appointed me a teacher in, and eventually superintendent of, his Sunday schools. This of course brought me into very close relations with the youth of the village, and especially with those who had been selected as choristers for the church. Among these latter I found two brothers, Lionel and Edgar St. Aubyn, who so evidently showed signs of a special musical talent that I offered to give them occasional instruction at my house to encourage them to develop it. Needless to say, they eagerly accepted the offer, and thus in time quite an attachment sprang up between us.

At this period I was much interested in the study of spiritualistic phenomena; and as I accidentally discovered that these two boys were good physical mediums, I had occasional quiet séances at my own house after the music lesson was over. Very curious some of our experiences were, but it is not of those I wish to speak now. I should mention that after these evening sittings it was my custom to walk home with my two choristers, who lived perhaps a mile and a half from my house.

Once, after such an evening, I had occasion to sit up writing until a late hour in the library where the sitting had taken place. I always observed that after a seance the furniture had an unpleasant way of creaking (sometimes even moving slightly at intervals) for some hours; and on this particular night this was specially noticeable. However, I wrote away, little heeding it, until about two o'clock, when suddenly, without being conscious of the slightest reason for doing so, I felt an uncontrollable impulse to go to my bedroom, which was close by. Wondering what this might mean, I laid down my pen, opened the door, and stepped out into the passage.

What was my surprise to see the door of my bedroom ajar, and a light shining from it, where I knew that no light ought to be! I promptly went to the door, and without pushing it further open, looked cautiously round it. What I saw so far astonished me as to keep me in that position for some little time, staring helplessly. Although there was no apparent source of light—nothing like a lamp or a candle—the room was full of a soft silvery radiance that made every object clearly visible. Nothing unfamiliar met my hasty glance around the room until it fell upon the bed; but there—and as I write I can feel again the sudden chill which crept down my back at the sight—there lay the form of Lionel St. Aubyn, whom I had seen safely enter his mother's house five hours before!

I am bound to admit that my first impulse was a most unheroic one—to slam the door and rush back headlong into my cosy library; however, I resisted it, mustered up my courage, pushed open the door a little further, and walked slowly to the foot of the bed. Yes, there he lay; unmistakably Lionel, and yet not looking in the least as I had ever seen him look before. His hands were crossed upon his breast, and his wide-open eyes looked full into mine, but with no ordinary expression; and though I had not till then seen it, I felt at once instinctively that their bright fixed gaze was that of supreme clairvoyant vision, and that the boy was in that highest state of ecstatic trance, which even great mesmerists can but rarely superinduce in their best subjects.

I thought I saw recognition come into his eyes, but there was not the slightest movement of face or limb; the spell seemed far too deep for that. He was dressed in a long white robe not unlike the ecclesiastical alb, and across his breast there was a broad crimson sash, edged and heavily embroidered with gold. The feelings with which I regarded this extraordinary apparition are more easily imagined than described; so prominent among them, I know, was the thought that surely I must be asleep, and dreaming all this, that I distinctly remember pinching my left arm, as men do in novels, to find out whether I was really awake. The result seemed to prove that I was, so I leaned my folded arms on the foot of the bedstead for a moment, trying to muster up courage to step forward and *touch* my unexpected guest.

But as I paused, a change seemed to take place in my surroundings; the walls of my room appeared somehow to expand, and suddenly—though still leaning on the foot of the bed, and still closely watching its mysterious occupant—I found that we were in the centre of some vast, gloomy temple, such as those of ancient Egypt, whose massive pillars stretched away on all sides, while its roof was so lofty as to be scarcely discernible in the dim religious light. As I looked round in astonishment I could just distinguish that the walls were covered with huge paintings (some at least of the figures being considerably above life-size) though the light was not strong enough to show them clearly. We were quite alone, and my wandering glance soon fixed itself again on the incredible presence of my entranced companion.

Now came an experience which I am aware it is difficult, if not impossible, for me to explain adequately. I can only say that I seemed to myself for the time being to have solved the problem of maintaining a conscious existence in two places at once; for while still gazing fixedly at Lionel inside the temple, I knew that I was also standing outside the same temple, in front of the grand entrance. A magnificent facade it was, apparently facing the west; for a great flight of broad black marble steps (fifty of them at least) which, extending the whole width of the building, led up to it from the plain, gleamed blood-red under the horizontal rays of the setting sun. I turned, and looked for surrounding habitations, but nothing was visible in any direction but one level unbroken desert of sand, save only three tall palm-trees in the distance on my right hand. Never till my dying day can I forget that weird, desolate picture—that limitless yellow desert, thesolitary clump of palm-trees, and that huge forsaken temple bathed in blood-red light.

Quickly this scene faded away, and I was inside again, though still preserving that strange double consciousness; for while one part of me still remained in its original posture, the other saw the wonderful paintings on the walls pass before it like the dissolving views of a magic lantern. Unfortunately I have never been able to recall clearly the subject of those pictures, but I know that they were of a most exciting nature, and that the figures were remarkably spirited and life-like. This exhibition seemed to last for some time; and then, quite suddenly, my consciousness was no longer divided, but once more concentrated itself where the visible body had been all the time—leaning with my folded arms on the foot of the bedstead gazing fixedly on the face of the boy.

As I stood there, bewildered, awe-stricken, a voice fell upon my ear with startling suddenness— quite a natural, ordinary voice, though it spoke clearly and emphatically.

"Lionel must not be mesmerized," it said; "it would kill him."

I looked round hastily, but no one was visible, and no further remark was made. Once again I pinched my arm, hoping to find myself dreaming; but no—the result was the same as ever, and I felt that the awe which was upon me would develope into ignoble fear unless I did something to break the spell; so with an effort I pulled myself together, and moved slowly along the side of the bed.

I stood directly over Lionel—I bent my head down till I was looking close into his face; but not a muscle moved, not a shadow of change came into the expression of those wonderful luminous eyes, and for some moments I remained spell-bound, breathless, my face within a few inches of his. Then by a mighty effort I shook off the controlling influence and grasped wildly at the figure before me. In a moment the light vanished, and I found myself in total darkness kneeling beside my own bed, and tightly grasping the counterpane with both hands!

I rose, gathered my scattered wits, and tried to persuade myself that I must have fallen asleep in my chair, dreamed an extraordinarily vivid dream, and in the course of it walked into my bedroom. I cannot say that even then I felt at all satisfied with this explanation, because my common sense assured me that it was all wrong; but at any rate I decided that I could do no more work that night, so I locked my desk, bathed my head with cold water, and went to bed.

Though I rose late the next morning, I still felt extremely weak and fatigued, which I attributed to the influence of my dream; however, I decided to say nothing about it, lest it should alarm my mother. I remember looking curiously in the broad daylight at the black marks made on my left arm by the pinches I had given myself in my dream.

That evening it chanced that Lionel St. Aubyn had to call at my house again—I forget now for what purpose; but I remember very distinctly that in course of conversation he suddenly said:

" O, sir, I had *such* a curious dream last night! "

A sort of electric shock ran through me at the words, but I retained sufficient presence of mind to say:

" Had you? Well, I am just coming out, so you can tell me about it as we walk along."

Even then I had some uneasy prevision of what was coming—enough at least to make me wish to get him out of earshot from my mother before he said any more. As soon as we were outside, I asked for particulars, and the cold thrill of last night ran down my spine when he began by saying:

"I dreamt, sir, that I was lying on a bed—not asleep, somehow, though I couldn't move hand or foot; but I could see quite well, and I had a strange feeling that I have never had before. I felt so wise, as though I could have answered any question in the world, if only some one had asked me."

"How did you lie, Lionel?" I asked him; and I could feel my hair rise gently as he answered:

"I lay on my back, with my hands crossed in front of me."

"I suppose you were dressed just as you are now?"

"O no, sir! I was dressed in a sort of long white gown, such as the priest wears under his chasuble; and across my breast and over one shoulder I had a broad band of red and gold; it looked so pretty, you can't think."

I knew only too well how it had looked, but I kept my thoughts to myself. Of course I saw by this time that my last night's expedition was more than an ordinary dream, and I felt that his experiences would prove to be the same as mine; but

I had a wild feeling of struggling against fate which prompted me to make every effort to find some difference, some flaw which would give me a loophole of escape from that conclusion; so I went on:

"You were in your own bedroom, of course?"

But he replied:

"No, sir; at first I was in a room that I thought I knew, and then suddenly it seemed to grow larger, and it was not a room at all, but a great strange temple, like the pictures I have seen in books, with great heavy pillars, and beautiful pictures painted on its walls."

"This was a very interesting dream, Lionel; tell me in what sort of city this temple stood."

It was quite useless; I could not mislead him. The inevitable answer came, as I knew it would:

"Not in a city at all, sir; it was in the middle of a great plain of sand, like the Sahara desert in our geography books; and I could see nothing but sand all round, except far away on the right three nice tall trees with no branches, such as we see in the pictures of Palestine."

"And what was your temple built of?"

"Of shining black stone, sir; but the great flight of steps in front looked all red, like fire, because of the sun shining on it."

"But how could you see all this when you were inside, boy?"

"Well, sir, I don't know; it was odd, but I seemed somehow to be outside and inside too; and though I could not move all the time, yet I seemed to go and look at all the beautiful pictures on the walls, but I could not understand how it was."

And now at last I asked the question that had been in my mind from the first—which I longed, yet dreaded, to put:

"Did you see any men in this strange dream, Lionel?"

"Yes, sir" (looking up brightly) "I saw *you*; only you, no other men."

I tried to laugh, though I am conscious it must have been but a feeble attempt, and asked what I had appeared to be doing.

"You came in sir, when I was in the room; you put your head round the door first, and when you saw me you looked so suprised, and stared at me ever so long; and then you came in, and walked slowly up to the foot of my bed. You took hold of your left arm with your right hand, and seemed to be pulling and pinching at it. Then you leaned your arms on the bedstead, and stood like that all the while we were in that strange temple, and while I saw the pictures. When they were gone, you took hold of your arm again, and then you came slowly along the side of the bed towards me. You looked so wild and strange that I was quite frightened."

('I have no doubt I did,' thought I, 'I certainly felt so.') "Then you came and stooped down till your face nearly touched mine, and still I could not move. Then suddenly you seemed to give a spring, and catch at me with your hands; and that woke me, and I found I was lying safe in my own bed at home."

As may readily be imagined, this exact confirmation of my own experience, and the strange way in which the boy had evidently seen me doing, even in the merest details, just what I seemed to myself to do, had a very eerie effect on my mind as it was poured out to me in innocent childish frankness, while we passed through the weird moonlight and the deep shadows of the great trees on that lonely road; but I endeavoured to confine myself to ordinary expressions of astonishment and interest, and to this day Lionel St. Aubyn has no idea how remarkable an experience his 'curious dream' really was.

I have stated these facts with scrupulous exactness just as they occurred. How are they to be explained? Two possibilities occur to me, but there are difficulties about both of them. The experience may be an instance of the phenomenon called double dreaming, wherein two persons have simultaneously exactly the same dream. It is probable that when that happens, only one of the persons really actively dreams, and the pictures which he sees or evokes are somehow reflected into the brain of the other, or even hypnotically impressed thereupon. In such cases the two partners in the experience usually see and do exactly the same things; but this time, though both saw the same objects and both had the singular experience of double consciousness, our actions were quite different, and each saw the other as that other imagined himself to be.

The other hypothesis is that Lionel was really in my room in his astral body, and that either he was materialized, or my sight was somehow temporarily opened so that I could see him; that we did actually somehow journey together in astral bodies through space to that forsaken temple in the far-off desert, and there go through together a very strange experience. This theory also presents difficulties, and to those who have never studied these matters it will appear far more improbable than the other; yet I myself believe it to be at least partially true. I believe that Lionel *was* brought astrally into my room, and that I really saw him there; though it is possible that the vision of the forsaken temple may then have been impressed upon us both by some will stronger than our own.

I have always had a suspicion that a third will *was* concerned in the affair, and that the words spoken by the mysterious voice were the *raison d'être* of the whole. For an adult member of the choir, who had heard of our successful seances, was keenly anxious to try his alleged mesmeric powers upon Lionel, asserting that so good a medium would probably be clairvoyant in trance. My instinct was strongly against this, though as I had no reason to give for it, I should probably have yielded to persuasion; but after this curious occurrence I refused quite definitely to sanction any experiment of that kind, holding that after such a warning it would be the height of folly. Now, the giving of that warning *may* have been the object of the vision, and all the rest of the display may have been simply intended to impress the order strongly on our minds —as it certainly did.

THE MAJOR'S PROMISE

THE story which I am about to relate is one of my earliest recollections, for I heard it many years ago from my great-grandfather. Though at the time of which I write he had passed by eight or nine years that limit of fourscore winters which is scripturally announced as the extreme period of human existence, he was an erect, soldierly old man still, and displayed not only a perfect retention of all his faculties, but a degree of both mental and physical vigour very unusual at so advanced an age—as may be inferred from the fact that he was in the habit of riding out daily until within three weeks of his death, which occurred at the age of ninety-two.

It will not, therefore, be open to the sceptic to dismiss my tale as distorted by the dreamy semi-recollection of dotage; nor, on the other hand, can he ignore it as exaggerated by the childish fancy of the listener. For I depend not on my own memory, but on a carefully-written account of the affair (dated in the year of its occurrence) found among the old man's papers after his death. It is fair to add that though it was not until some twenty years later that I had an opportunity of perusing this paper, I found it to agree in every particular with my own vivid recollection of the story.

That written account I reproduce almost literally, supplying from my memory only some few details of the conversations, and of course altering the names of all the actors. I remember that my great-grandfather used to tell us that some author (he forgot the name) called upon one of the friends who shared this experience with him, and begged to be allowed to take down his deposition to the facts of the case. It must have been in this way that the story came to be included in Mrs. Catherine Crowe's remarkable book *The Night Side of Nature*. It appears there in a much curtailed form, omitting many of the phenomena here related. This, then, was the old man's tale:

When I was a youngster I entered as a cadet into the service of the Honourable East India Company, and set sail from Plymouth one fine morning in the good ship *Somerset*, with several other young fellows who were eastward bound on the same errand as myself. Those were stirring times, and many a vision of glory to be won on the battle-field floated before our youthful eyes. A merry company we were, for they were good fellows all—gay, light-hearted, and careless; and so with story, jest, and song we did our best to make the long hours of that tedious voyage pass as rapidly as we could.

One among my comrades had a peculiar attraction for me, perhaps because he alone of all the party seemed to have occasional fits of sadness—spells of serious thought, during which he withdrew into himself, and almost repelled the advances of his companions. He was a young Highlander named Cameron, handsome, dark, and tall, a well-read man but one who shrank from displaying his knowledge; a man somewhat out of the ordinary run, one felt instinctively—a man, perhaps, with a history.

As I said, he had a peculiar attraction for me, and though he was reserved at first, we ultimately became firm friends; and in his more melancholy moods, when he avoided the society of others, he yet seemed to find a sort of passive pleasure in mine. At such times he would say but little, but would sit for an hour gazing steadily at the horizon, with a strange far-away look in his deep, earnest eyes. So would a man look (I often thought) whom some terrible sorrow, some ghastly experience, had marked off for ever from the rest of his kind; but I asked no questions. I waited patiently till the time should come when our ripening friendship would reveal the secret.

One thing more I noticed; that whenever the conversation turned, as it did several times during the voyage, upon what is commonly called the supernatural (a subject upon which most of us were derisively sceptical, as was the fashion in those days) my friend not only expressed no opinion whatever, but invariably withdrew himself from the party or contrived to change the subject. No one else, however, appeared to notice this, and I said nothing about it.

Well, in due course we arrived at Madras and, after staying there about a fortnight, five of us, including my friend Cameron and myself, received orders to join our regiment at an up-country station. Our party was under the charge of a certain Major Rivers, whom, during the short time we had known him, we had all learnt to like very much. He was a small, spare man, with short-sighted grey eyes and a peculiarly pleasant smile; a man of extreme punctuality in trifles, but frank, kindly, and genial; a thorough soldier and a thorough sportsman. Indeed, his devotion to sport had left its mark upon him in the shape of a very perceptible limp, the result of an accident in the hunting-field.

A considerable part of our journey had to be performed by water, so a kind of barge was put into requisition for us, and we started at day-break one morning. It soon grew insufferably hot, the country was flat, and our progress extremely slow, so you will not be surprised to hear that we found the time hang somewhat heavily upon our hands. Sometimes we got out and walked a few yards to stretch our legs, but the heat of the sun soon drove us under our awning again. By the evening of the second day we were in a state of *ennui* bordering on desperation, when the Major suddenly said with a smile:

"Gentlemen, I have a proposal to make."

"Hear, hear!" we all shouted; "anything to vary this detestable monotony!"

"My idea," said the Major, "is this. You see that little hill over there to the right? Well, I know this part of the country thoroughly, and I know that the river passes just on the other side of that hill. Now though it is, as you see, only a few miles off in a straight line, it is at least four times that distance by water, in consequence of the windings of the river. We are now about to stop for the night, and I thought that if we left the boat here to-morrow morning, arranging to meet it again in the evening at the base of that hill, we might relieve the tedium of the journey by a little shooting in those jungles, where I know from experience there is good sport to be had."

Of course we hailed the suggestion with acclamation, and at an early hour the next morning we took our guns and leapt ashore, accompanied by a large dog which belonged to one of the party—a

fine, intelligent animal, and a general favourite.
The Major had created some amusement by ap-
pearing in an enormous pair of top-boots, many
sizes too large for him; but when some one suggested that he seemed more prepared for fishing than
shooting, he only laughed good-naturedly and said
that before the day was over we might perhaps
wish that we had been as well protected as he was.
In sooth he was right, for we found the ground for
some distance decidedly marshy, and in many
places, to obtain a footing at all, we had to spring
from bush to bush and stone to stone in a way that,
encumbered as we were with our guns, soon made
us most unpleasantly warm. At last our difficulties
culminated in a muddy stream or ditch which
looked about twelve feet broad.

"Rather a long jump for a man with a heavy
gun!" I said.

"Oh," replied the Major, "I think we can
manage it; at any rate I am going to try, and if I
get òver with my game leg, it ought to be easy
enough for you young fellows."

He took a short run, and sprang, just clearing
the ditch; but unluckily the slimy edge of the bank
gave way under his feet, and he slipped back into
the water. In a moment the rest of us took the
leap, all getting safely across, and rushed to his
assistance. He was quite unhurt, and, thanks to

the enormous top-boots, not even wet; but his gun was choked with mud, and required a thorough cleaning. He threw himself down with a laugh under the nearest tree, and began fanning himself with his hat, saying:

"You will have to go on without me for awhile."

We protested against leaving him, objecting that we did not know the country, and offered to stop and help him; but this he refused to permit.

"No, no," he said, "you must push on, and see what you can find; I shall follow in half an hour or so. We cannot miss one another, and at the worst there is always the hill as a landmark, so you have only to climb a tree and you will get the direction at once. But in any case do not fail to be at the boat at five o'clock, for whether I overtake you in the meantime or not, *I promise you I will be there to meet you.*"

Somewhat reluctantly we obeyed, and plunged into the jungle, leaving him still lying fanning himself under the tree. We had walked on for about an hour without much success, and were just beginning to wonder when the Major would join us, when Cameron, who happened to be next to me, stopped suddenly, turned pale as death, and pointing straight before him cried in accents of horror:

"See! see! merciful heaven, look there!"

"Where? what? what is it?" we all shouted confusedly, as we rushed up to him and looked round in expectation of encountering a tiger, a cobra, we hardly knew what, but assuredly something terrible, since it had been sufficient to cause such evident emotion in our usually self-contained comrade. But neither tiger nor cobra was visible; nothing but Cameron, pointing with ghastly haggard face and starting eyeballs at *something we could not see*.

"Cameron! Cameron!" cried I, seizing his arm, "for heaven's sake, speak! what is the matter?"

Scarcely were the words out of my mouth when a low but very peculiar sound struck on my ear, and Cameron, dropping his pointing hand, said in a hoarse strained voice:

"There! you heard it? Thank God it's over!"

Even as he spoke he fell to the ground insensible. There was a momentary confusion while we unfastened his collar, and I dashed in his face some water which I fortunately had in my flask, while another tried to pour brandy between his clenched teeth; and under cover of it I whispered to the man next me (one of our greatest sceptics, by the way):

"Beauchamp, did *you* hear anything?"

"Why, yes," he replied, "a curious sound, very; a sort of crash or rattle far away in the distance, yet very distinct; if the thing were not utterly impossible I could have sworn it was the rattle of musketry."

"Just my impression," murmured I; "but hush! he is recovering."

In a minute or two he was able to speak feebly, and began to thank us and apologize for giving trouble; and soon he sat up, leaning against a tree, and in a firm though still low voice said:

"My dear friends, I feel I owe you an explanation of my extraordinary behaviour. It is an explanation that I would fain avoid giving; but it must come some time, and so may as well be given now.

"You may perhaps have noticed that when during the voyage you all joined in scoffing at dreams, portents, and visions, I invariably avoided giving any opinion on the subject. I did so because, while I had no desire to court ridicule or provoke discussion, I was unable to agree with you, knowing only too well from my own dread experience that the world which men agree to call that of the supernatural is just as real as this world we see about us —perhaps even far more so. In other words, I, like many of my countrymen, am cursed with the gift of second sight—that awful faculty which foretells in vision calamities that are shortly to occur.

" Such a vision I had just now, and its exception-
al horror moved me as you have seen. I saw before
me a corpse—not that of one who has died a peace-
ful, natural death, but that of the victim of some
terrible accident—a ghastly, shapeless mass, with a
face swollen, crushed, unrecognizable. I saw this
dreadful object placed in a coffin, and the funeral
service performed over it; I saw the burial-ground,
I saw the clergymen; and though I had never seen
either before, I can picture both perfectly in my
mind's eye now. I saw you, myself, Beauchamp,
all of us and many more, standing round as mour-
ners; I saw the soldiers raise their muskets after the
service was over; I heard the volley they fired—and
then I knew no more."

As he spoke of that volley of musketry I glanced
across with a shudder at Beauchamp, and the look
of stony horror on that handsome sceptic's face was
one not to be forgotten. The spell of the vision was
upon us all, and no one liked to be the first to
speak; and for a long minute, perhaps two minutes,
there was a silence which could be felt—that silence
of tropical noon which is so far deeper than that of
midnight.

And then—it was broken. Broken, not by any of
the ordinary sounds of the forest, but by one which
under the circumstances startled us far more than
the growl of the tiger or the hiss of the serpent would

have done—the deep solemn 'clang!' of a great church-bell.

"Good God, what is that?" cried Beauchamp, thoroughly unnerved, as we all sprang to our feet, while the dog threw up his head and howled.

"It's the bell tolling for that funeral of Cameron's", said Granville, the wit of our party, trying to smile with a very white face; but I doubt if ever a joke fell flatter, for we were in no mood for laughter. While we still stood awe-stricken, gazing at one another, again the unmistakable sonorous 'clang!' rang out in our ears—not borne by the wind and mellowed by distance, but in the very midst of us, close over our heads—so close that we felt the ground vibrate in response to its stroke.

"Let us leave this accursed spot!" cried I, seizing Cameron's arm, Beauchamp caught him by the other, and between us we half supported, half dragged him along. The others followed; but we had not gone ten yards before that hollow knell sounded once more in our midst, adding wings to our speed; and again the dog howled dismally.

Nothing else happened, however, and for a mile or more we hurried along in silence, until we came upon a beautiful grassy dell through which meandered a clear silvery streamlet. On its edge we threw ourselves down to rest; indeed Cameron, not yet thoroughly recovered, seemed incapable of going further. After a long draught of the cool water we became more composed, and began seriously to review our late remarkable experience.

As to Cameron's vision, after witnessing his intense and painful agitation it was impossible to doubt that it was sufficiently real to him, and (the phenomenon being a purely subjective one) there was little more to be said. More difficult to deal with was the faint, distant, yet surprisingly distinct sound of volley of musketry which Beauchamp and I had both heard. Granville and Johnson, who had heard nothing, declared that the sound had existed only in our heated imagination, excited as we naturally were by Cameron's strange condition; and when reminded of its singular agreement with the termination of his vision attributed that fact to mere coincidence.

Neither Beauchamp nor I were at all satisfied with this; we had heard the sound, and we knew that this theory was not the true explanation; but as we were entirely unable to suggest a more rational one, it was useless to argue. But then that weird church-bell! No one dreamt of suggesting imagination in that case; we had all alike heard it—all felt the vibration of the earth which it caused—all agreed exactly in the description of its sound, and in locating it in the very midst of us.

"Still," said Granville, " of course there must be some means of accounting for it naturally.

Even if there were such things as spirits, it would be absurd to suppose them capable of producing a noise such as that. I have read of cases in which some unusual description of echo has been found capable of reproducing a sound with startling fidelity even at an almost incredible distance."

"An echo!" replied Cameron scornfully; "there is not a church-bell within fifty miles of us—not such an one as that, probably, in the whole of India, for it sounded like the Great Bell of Moscow."

"Yes, that sound had certainly not travelled fifty miles," remarked Beauchamp reflectively. "You have heard, I suppose, of the *campanero* of South America?"

We had all read of this lovely bird and its wonderful bell-like note, but we had no reason to believe that any such creature existed in India; besides, we all agreed that no specimen of the feathered tribe was ever hatched which could have produced that tremendous metallic clang.

"I wish the Major had been with us," said Granville; "he knows the country, and perhaps he might be able to suggest something. Ha! I have it! I see the explanation of the mystery! How absurd of us not to have thought of it before! Of course the Major, who stayed behind, has been playing some trick upon us, and is now having a good laugh somewhere or other at the recollection of our foolish fright!"

"A bright idea! that must be it!" exclaimed Beauchamp and Johnson together.

"But stay," interposed I, "*how* could he have done it? He can hardly have been carrying a bell weighing two or three tons or so in his coatpocket."

"Oh, no doubt he found some method or other," answered Granville; "for example, I have heard that a properly prepared bar of iron will when struck give out a very fair imitation of a bell sound."

"Perhaps so, but then properly prepared bars of iron are not usually to be found lying about in an Indian jungle, and he certainly brought nothing with him from the boat."

"Well, possibly the barrel of his gun might be made—" but here a general smile checked the speaker, and Cameron quietly remarked:

"No, Granville, I do not think that will quite answer as an explanation; besides, how do you account for the sound coming from a point close above our heads?"

"Much may be done by skilful management of ventriloquism", replied Granville.

"Ventriloquism! my dear fellow, can you seriously suppose that such a sound as that ever proceeded from any human throat?"

"Well," answered Granville, "I cannot say; but until you can find me a better, I cling to my hypothesis that the Major is responsible for our fright in some way or other."

To this Beauchamp and Johnson somewhat hesitatingly agreed; Cameron smiled sadly and shook his head, but said no more; as for myself, I knew not what to think, for my scepticism was considerably shaken by the strange events of the morning.

We lay there by that pleasant stream for some hours, each ransacking his memory in turn for some half-forgotten story of the supernatural, of goblin, ghost, or fairy, told perhaps by some old nurse in happy childish days. The only tale that dwells in my recollection is a short one told by Cameron in answer to a question as to his first experience of the faculty of second sight.

"The first experience I well remember," he said; "I was a little lad of six or seven, and one evening when my father and I were out walking together, we stood to watch the fishermen of our little village push off their boats and start for their night's work. Among them were two fine lads, Alec and Donald, who were particular favourites of mine, and used frequently to bring strange fish for "the little laird" (as they called me) to see; and once I had even been out in their boat. So I waved my hand to them as they set sail, and then we continued our ramble, ascending the cliffs so that we could watch the boats as they stood far out to sea.

"We were nearly at home again, coming round an angle of the grey old castle wall, I was much surprised to see Alec and Donald leaning against it. I was about to speak to them, when the sudden tightening of my father's grasp upon my hand caused me to look up in his face, and the stern, set expression that I saw there diverted my attention for the moment from the lads, though I noticed they did not give us the customary salute—in fact, did not seem to see us at all.

"'Father,' I asked, 'what can Alec and Donald be doing there?'

"He looked down on me with deep compassion, and said:

"'And did ye see them too? Eh! my lad, my lad!'

"After that he took no notice of my question, and spoke no more till we reached home. He retired to his room, while I ran down to the beach to see why my young friends' boat had returned; but to my astonishment there was no boat there, and an old woman, who had been sitting spinning at her door close by the whole time, assured me that there certainly had been none since the whole fleet set sail together two hours before. I was puzzled, but still I never doubted that somehow my friends had been there in real flesh and blood; even the great storm which woke me in the night suggested nothing, and it was only when in the early morning I saw men reverently bearing two bodies into the house where Alec and Donald had lived, that I had any idea of the true nature of what I had seen."

Thus time passed on, till the declining rays of the sun warned us that we must think of returning to the boat. We had not far to go, for the hill at whose foot we were to meet was full in sight, and we had only to pass through a wood which skirted its base. By this time we had somewhat recovered our normal tone, and were laughing and chatting gaily, wondering where we should find the Major, and thinking what an incredible story we had to tell him. Beauchamp, who was leading, called out:

" Here is the end of the wood at last! "

Suddenly his dog, which had been roaming about in advance, came flying back and cowered down among us with every sign of excessive fear. We had no time to wonder at this unusual behaviour before again in our midst sounded that solemn sonorous ' clang! ' just as before, and again the trembling dog threw up his head and howled.

" Ha! " exclaiming Cameron, quickly turning upon Granville; "echo? ventriloquism? an iron

6

bar? a musket-barrel? which hypothesis do you prefer now? "

And as his voice ceased the dread unearthly knell again crashed forth. With one consent we sprang towards the open ground at the end of the wood, but before we could reach it the spectral bell rang once more in our very ears—almost in our very brains, as it seemed—amid the frantic howls of the dog. We rushed out in great disorder into the broad meadow sloping down to the river, and it was with an unutterable sense of relief that we saw our boat, already moored, waiting to receive us, and the Major some distance in front of us limping hastily towards it.

" Major! Major! " we shouted.

But he did not turn his head, sharp though his ears were generally; he only hurried on towards the boat, so we all started in pursuit, running as hard as we could. To our surprise the dog, instead of accompanying us, uttered one final dismal yelp and dashed back into the haunted wood; but no one thought of following him, for our attention was fixed on the Major. Fast as we ran we were unable to overtake him, and we were still some fifty yards from the boat when he hurried across the plank that the boatman had just put down as a gangway. He went down the stairs, still in the same hurried manner, and we rushed after him, but to our intense surprise were unable to find him anywhere. The door of his cabin stood wide open, but it was empty; and though we searched the whole barge, not a trace of him could we find.

"Well," cried Granville, "this is the strangest trick of all."

Cameron and I exchanged glances, but Granville, not observing us, rushed on deck and demanded of the head boatman where the Major was.

"Sahib," replied the man. "I have not seen him since he left with you this morning."

"Why, what do you mean?" roared Granville; "he came on board this barge not a minute before we did, and I saw you put down a plank for him to cross with your own hands!"

"Sir," answered the man, exhibiting the greatest astonishment, 'you certainly mistake; you were yourself the first person to come on board, and I laid down the plank because I saw you coming; as for the Major Sahib, I have not set eyes upon him since morning."

We could do nothing but stare at one another in blank amazement, not unmingled with awe; and I heard Cameron mutter as if to himself:

"He *is* dead, then, as I feared, and the vision was for him after all."

"There is something very strange about all this," said Beauchamp, "something which I cannot at all understand; but one thing is clear. We must at once go back to the place where we left the Major this morning, and search for him. Some accident may have happened."

We explained to the head boatman where we had parted from the Major, and found that he at once shared our worst fears.

"That is a very dangerous place, Sahib," he said; "there was once a village there, and there are two or three deep wells whose mouths are entirely overgrown by bushes and weeds; and the Major Sahib, being so short-sighted, would be very likely to fall into one of them."

This intelligence naturally increased our apprehensions tenfold, and we lost no time in setting off, taking with us three of the boatmen and a coil of stout rope. As may be imagined, it was not without a shudder that we plunged again into the wood where we had heard those mysterious sounds which we had now so much reason to fear might have been in some inexplicable way intended as warnings to us of a calamity impending, or perhaps even then taking place. But the conversation turned chiefly on the latest marvel—the appearance and disappearance of what we could hardly help calling the Major's ghost.

We carefully compared notes, and ascertained beyond a doubt that all five of us had clearly seen him. We had all observed his hurried manner; we had all noticed that, though still wearing the top-boots, he had no hat upon his head and was no longer carrying his gun; we had all seen him descend the stairs on board the boat, and we were all perfectly certain that it would have been impossible for him, if a man in the flesh, to escape us unobserved. Sceptics though some of us had been as to supernatural visitations, I think none of us now ventured to hope that we should find him alive; and perhaps it is no discredit to our prowess as soldiers to confess that we kept very close together as we retraced our steps through those woods, and that we spoke chiefly in whispers, except when at intervals we stopped, let off our pieces, and all shouted together, so that if the Major were lying disabled anywhere in the neighbourhood he would be aware of our approach.

However, we met with nothing unusual on our way, and found without difficulty the place where we had crossed the ditch, and the tree under which we had left the Major. From this spot the boatmen easily tracked his footsteps for a few hundred yards, till one of them, running forward, picked up the hat and gun of the missing man—" the very articles," whispered Cameron to me, " which he had not when we saw him just now." We now felt certain that some terrible accident had occurred—

probably close to the very spot where we stood; and sure enough the natives pointed out to us only a few yards off the concealed mouth of one of those old wells of which they had warned us. Alas! at its edge there were the unmistakable marks of slipping feet; and from the blackness of the depth into which we looked, we could hardly doubt that our poor friend must have been fatally injured, even if not at once killed, by the fall.

The sun was already setting, and night comes on so rapidly in the tropics that we had but little time to lose; so, as no answer came to our shouts, we hastily passed our rope round the branch of a tree which hung over the mouth of the well, and by its means one of the boatmen descended. Soon from an immense depth a shout came up; the man had reached the bottom, and had discovered a body, but was unable to tell us whether it was the Major's or not. We directed him to attach it to the rope, and with fast-beating hearts drew it to the surface of the earth.

Never shall I forget the ghastly sight that met our eyes in the rapidly-fading light. The corpse was indeed the Major's, but it was only by the clothes and the top-boots that we could identify it; scarcely anything of human shape was left in it, and the face was swollen and crushed past all recognition, as Cameron had seen it in his vision.

Death must have been instantaneous, for evidently as he fell down the well, the head must have struck more than once against the rough rocky projections which we could see as we peered into it. Horrible to relate, entangled in the rope which had been so hurriedly tied round the corpse was also the mangled, but yet warm and palpitating body of *Beauchamp's dog*, which had rushed so madly into the jungle but an hour before! Sick with horror we twined together a rude litter of branches, laid the Major's remains upon it with averted eyes, and bore it silently back to our boat.

So ends my gruesome story, and few will wonder that a permanent effect was produced upon the life of each one of its witnesses. Since then I have borne my part in many a battle-field, and faced death calmly enough in its most dreadful forms (for familiarity breeds contempt); but yet there are times when that unearthly bell, that spectral figure, that awful corpse rise once more before my mind, and a great horror falls upon me, and I dread to be alone.

One more fact I ought to mention to make my tale complete. When, on the following evening, we arrived at our destination, and our melancholy deposition had been taken down by the proper authorities, Cameron and I went out for a quiet walk, to endeavour with the assistance of the soothing influence of nature to shake off something of the gloom which paralysed our spirits. Suddenly he clutched my arm, and pointing through some rude railings, said in a trembling voice:

"Yes, there it is! that is the burial-ground I saw yesterday."

And when later on we were introduced to the chaplain of the post, I noticed, though my friends did not, the irrepressible shudder with which Cameron took his hand, and I knew that he had recognized the clergyman of his vision.

———

Such is my great-grandfather's story. As for its occult rationale, I presume Cameron's vision to have been a pure case of second sight, and if so, the fact that the two men who were evidently nearest to him (certainly one and probably both actually *touching* him) participated in it to the limited extent of hearing the concluding volley while the others who were not so close did not, would show that the intensity with which the vision impressed itself upon the seer occasioned a disturbance in his aura which was communicated to that of each person in contact with him, as in ordinary thought-transference.

The bell sounds seem to have been an exceedingly powerful manifestation, probably produced by the dead Major, as an attempt to apprise his friends of the accident which had befallen him. It frequently happens that a dead man, unaccustomed to his new surroundings and unacquainted with the methods of wielding super-physical forces, plunges wildly about in his desperate efforts to communicate somehow with the world that he has left, and in doing so produces results as unexpected to himself as to his friends on earth. I have not heard of another instance of their taking exactly this form, but I have heard of others quite as tremendous; so I agree with Granville in holding the Major responsible for that weird signal, though I do not know exactly how he caused it.

From what we hear of the Major's extreme punctuality, it is probable that the idea of keeping his promise to reach the boat at the time arranged may have been prominent in his mind immediately before death, and that prominent idea is enough to account for the apparition. The fact that the officers all saw it, and the boat-men did not, might be attributed to the intense excitement under which the former were labouring, in addition to the fact that they, as constant companions, would be much more *en rapport* with the deceased. The dog, as often happens, realized the character of the appearance sooner than the men did; but perhaps the most extraordinary point of the whole story is the discovery of its body along with the Major's. I can only suppose that in an additional attempt to turn the attention of his friends in the right direction, the Major may have drawn *it* back to the scene of the accident, though he could not draw *them*, and being unable to check itself in its headlong rush, it met with its death as he had done; but I offer this only as a conjecture.

A TEST OF COURAGE

How long I had slept I cannot say; but in a moment, with the suddenness of a flash of lightning, I passed from unconsciousness to complete and vivid consciousness. I gave a quick glance round my chamber; everything was visible clearly enough in the subdued light of my lamp, turned low for the night. All seemed as usual—nothing out of place, nothing to account in any way for that sudden awakening.

But the next moment there thrilled through my soul the well-known voice of that Teacher whom I revere and love above all else in the world. That voice uttered but one word:

"Come!"

Ere I could spring from my couch in glad obedience I was seized with a feeling which it would be hopeless to attempt to describe so as to give any one else an adequate conception of it. Every nerve in my body seemed strained to the breaking-point by some hitherto-unsuspected force within; after a moment of excruciating pain this sensation focussed itself in the upper part of the head, something there seemed to burst, and—I found myself floating in the air! One glance I cast behind me, and saw myself—or my body rather—lying soundly asleep upon the bed; and then I soared out into the open air.

It was a dark tempestuous night, and lowering clouds were driving rapidly across the sky; and it seemed to me as if the whole air were full of living creatures, shadowy and indistinctly seen through the darkness—creatures like wreaths of mist or smoke, and yet somehow living and powerful—creatures which seemed perpetually rushing towards me and yet retired before me; but I swept on unheeding.

The room in which I had been sleeping is on the bank of a river, and across this my flight tended. At this point there is in the centre of the stream a small islet—little more than a sandbank, half-covered when the water is high; and on this islet I alighted. Suddenly I found standing beside me the form of my mother, who had passed from this life some six years before.

" What is this? " I cried in amazement.

" Hush," said she, " *look there!* "

She pointed to the river whose waves washed almost to our feet. I looked, and saw a sight that might well have made the boldest tremble. Approaching us along the river was a vast army of enormous creatures such as man's wildest imagination could never conceive. I quite despair of giving any idea of the appearance of this huge mass of advancing horrors; perhaps the prevailing types might be described as resembling the pictures we see of the gigantic monsters of the so-called antediluvian era, and yet were far more fearful than they. Dark as the night was, I could see the hellish host clearly enough, for they had a light of their own; a strange unearthly luminosity seemed to emanate from each of them.

"Do you know what those are?" asked my mother in a voice of terror.

"Elements, are they not?" said I.

"Yes," she replied, "terrible elements of deadly power! Let us fly!"

But even in this crisis of horror I did not forget my Teacher's instructions, so I answered:

"No; I will never fly from an elemental; besides, it would be quite useless."

"Come with me," she cried; "better die a thousand deaths than fall into their power!"

"I will not fly", I repeated; and she rose hurriedly into the air and vanished.

To say that I was not abjectly frightened would be an untruth, but I certainly had not the courage to turn my back on that appalling army, and moreover I felt that flight from such power would be hopeless; my one chance was to endeavour to stand firm. By this time the advancing host was close at hand; but the first rank, instead of springing upon me as I expected, writhed slowly along in front of me in hideous procession. No such sight, assuredly, has ever been seen by man's physical eye; delirium itself could never give birth to horrors so unutterable as these.

Ichthyosauri, plesiosauri, prodigious batrachians, gigantic cuttlefish, sea-spiders twenty feet high, cobras of the size of the mythical sea-serpent, monsters shaped almost like some huge bird, yet obviously reptilian in character, ghastly bloodless creatures like enormously magnified animalculæ—all these and many more nameless variants defiled before my eyes; and yet no two of the obscene host were alike, and none seemed perfect; each had some peculiar and awful deformity of its own. But through all these diversities of form, each more inconceivably loathsome than the last, there ran a still more frightful likeness; and I soon realized that this likeness was in their *eyes*.

No matter what unclean shape each hateful monstrosity might bear, all alike had fiery, malignant eyes; and in every case in these baleful orbs there dwelt an awful demoniac power of fascination—an expression of bitter unrelenting hostility to the human race. Each noisome abomination, as it writhed slowly past, fixed its fearful eyes on mine, and seemed to be exerting some formidable power against me. How my reason retained its throne under these terrible conditions I shall never know; I felt somehow certain that if I once gave way to my fears I should instantly fall a victim to this demon host, and I concentrated all my being in the one faculty of stubborn resistance.

How long that terrific procession took to pass me I know not, but last of the loathly legion came a *something* which wore partly the semblance of a three-headed snake, though immeasurably greater than any earthly ophidian, and yet—oh horror! its heads and eyes seemed somehow human, or rather diabolical. And this dreadful misshapen THING, instead of gliding slowly past as the others had done, turned aside, and with raised crests and open mouths made straight at me! On it came, its blazing eyes fixed on mine, and blood-red slime or foam dropping from its enormous wide-open jaws, while I summoned up all my will-power for one last stupendous effort.

But that I clenched my hands and set my teeth hard, I moved no muscle, although the pestilent effluvium of its burning breath came full in my face —although in its onward rush it splashed the water over my feet, and even dropped its loathsome slime upon them; for I felt that life, and more than life, depended upon the strength of my will. How long that tremendous strain lasted I cannot say; but just as it seemed that I could hold out no longer I felt the resistance weaken; the fire died out of the fiendish eyes that were held so close to mine, and with a horrible roar of baffled rage the unclean monster fell back into the water! The whole troop had vanished, and I was alone in the dark night as at first.

But before the revulsion of feeling had time to set in, clear and sweet above my head rang the well-known astral bell, and I felt myself rising and moving swiftly through the air. In a moment I was back again in my own room, saw my body still lying in the same position, and with a sort of shock found myself one with it once more. But as I raised myself on my couch, I saw laid upon my bosom a lovely white lotus-blossom freshly plucked, with the dew still on the petals.

With heart throbbing with delight I turned towards the light to examine it more closely, when a puff of cold air drew my attention to the fact that my feet were wet, and looking down at them, I was horror-stricken to see that they were covered with splashes of some viscous red liquid! Instantly I rushed out to the bathroom and washed them again and again, finding it very difficult to get rid of the filthy treacly fluid, and when at last I was satisfied I went back to my room and sat down to admire my lotus-blossom, marvelling greatly.

Now, before lying down again to sleep, I have thus written this account of what happened to me, lest to-morrow I should fail to recollect any of the points clearly, though indeed there seems little fear of that, for they are burnt into my brain.

———

Later. My wonderful story is not yet quite finished. After writing thus far I lay down and slept, and was so weary that, contrary to my custom, I did not wake until after sunrise. The first object on which my eye fell was my lotus-blossom in the cup of water in which I had placed it before writing; and by the clearer light of day I discerned some reddish stains at the foot of the sheet on which I had lain. Rising, I determined to plunge into the river and swim across, so as to view by the morning light the scene of this strange nocturnal adventure. There lay the islet—there were the low level banks, just as I had seen them then; and yet by the clear morning sunshine it was difficult to put upon this stage the ghastly *dramatis personae* that occupied it last night.

I swam out to the sandbank, for it seemed to me that I could identify the very spot where I stood

7

during that terrible trial. Yes, here surely it must be, and—powers above us! what is this? Here are *footprints* in the sand—two deep footprints, side by side, made evidently by one who stood long and firmly in one position; no others leading up to them either from the water or from the other side of the islet; only just those two footprints—*my* footprints undoubtedly, for I try them and they fit exactly. And once more—what is this? Here on the sand, close by the footprints, I find traces still left of the horrible viscous liquid—the foul red slime that fell from the jaws of that elemental dragon!

I have thought over every possible hypothesis, and I cannot escape the conclusion that my experience was a real one. I did not walk in my sleep to make those footprints, for to reach the islet I must have swum some distance, and then not my feet only, but my whole body and clothes, must have been wet; and besides, that theory would hardly account for the slime and the lotus. But what of the female figure which I saw? I can only suppose it to have been a nature-spirit who had either seized upon the shell of my departed relative or for some reason had assumed her appearance.

Now, immediately on my return from the swim, I have made this addition to my narrative.

AN ASTRAL MURDER

What the Old Station-Master Told Me

Curious things, sir? Indeed, you're right there; I've heard and seen many of them in my time. There's not a man who has been in railway work for forty years, as I have, but could tell you tales— aye, and every word of them true, too—which beat anything you ever read in print. But railway men mostly work hard and say little and so the world rarely hears of them. Ghost stories? Yes, we know something about them too, but I don't greatly care to talk about *them*, for folks who think they know everything are apt to laugh, and that annoys me. Do I believe in them? Well, sir, since you ask me a plain question I'll give you a plain answer—I do; and that you may not think me a foolish fellow, if you have a few minutes to spare I'll tell you a story that will show why I do.

You remember that dreadful accident some years ago at Keysborough, two stations down the line? Ah, I forgot, it was before you came into this neighbourhood; but still you must have read of it in the papers; a sad affair it was, to be sure. It is of the day on which that happened that I have to speak. The third of July it was, I remember, and as lovely a morning as ever I saw in my life; little I thought as I stood at this door and enjoyed it, what a black day it would turn out for so many.

Well, you must know, sir, that shortly before that time there was on this part of the line an express driver named Tom Price, who drove the *Fire Queen*— one of the finest engines our company owned. You know a driver makes his way up gradually as he learns his work. First he drives a shunting engine, then a goods train, then a slow passenger train, then a fast train; and last of all, if he proves himself a thoroughly good man for the work, they put him in charge of one of the express engines. Very proud some of the men are of their engines, too; they seem to look upon them almost like living creatures; and in his own way I believe Tom Price was deeply attached to his *Fire Queen*, and would have felt any harm that occurred to her as though it had happened to himself.

A tall, dark, heavy fellow was Tom, stern and moody-looking; unsociable, a man of few words, and one who made no friends, though no one had any complaint against him; but a steady and careful man, always reliable where his work was concerned. It was said up in the yard that, though not easily roused, his temper was terrible when once excited, and that he never forgave those who offended him. There was a story told of his lying in wait for three days for a man who had seriously annoyed him in some way, and being with difficulty prevented from killing him by those who stood round; but I can't say how much of it was true.

It was little enough I knew of him, yet perhaps I was as much his friend as anybody, for each day I used to say a few cheery words to him as he stopped here till presently he got to give me a smile and a word or two in return; and when I heard he was courting black-eyed Hetty Hawkins whose father kept the level crossing a few miles down the line, just this side of Keysborough, I ventured to joke him about it, which I don't think any one else dared to do. Presently he was promoted to the express engine, and then I saw less of him than ever —or rather spoke less to him, for I was generally on the platform each morning to give him a wave of the hand as he ran the first quick train down; and sometimes I saw him again for a moment as he returned at night.

He had not been many months at his new work when there began to be some talk of pretty Hetty Hawkins having another suitor—a young carpenter named Joe Brown. I heard it first from one of the goods guards one morning, while his train was waiting on the siding for Tom's express to go by; and from the black look on Tom's face as he went through, we both thought that he had perhaps heard it too. This Joe Brown was generally held to be a worthless sort of young fellow; but then he was young and good-looking, and naturally his work gave him many more opportunities of hanging about after a girl than an engine-driver's did, so I felt it was rather hard on my poor friend Tom; for though it may be all very well to sing " Absence makes the heart grow fonder ", as far as *my* experience goes I've found a deal more truth in the old proverb " Out of sight, out of mind."

One trick of Joe's I must mention specially, since my story partly turns upon it. Hetty had been what is called strictly brought up—always kept steadily to school and church as a child; and even now she went regularly to a bible-class that the Rector of Keysborough held every Sunday morning for the young people of the parish—he taking the lads, and his wife the girls. Well, what does graceless Joe do—he who was not seen in a place of worship once in three months—but suddenly become extremely religious and join the Rector's bible-class! Of course his motives may have been perfectly pure, but gossips did sometimes whisper that the pleasure of walking through the dewy fields to the

Rectory and back with pretty Hetty Hawkins might perhaps have something to do with his sudden conversion.

Meanwhile I wondered what Tom Price thought of all this; but I had no chance to speak to him until one morning, owing to some delay in shunting, it happened that the signals were against him, and he had to draw up for a few moments at the platform.

"Tom," said I, " is this true what I hear about Joe Brown courting your Hetty? "

"Aye," he replied with an oath and a frown, "it's true enough, I am afraid; but if ever I catch the fellow near her he had better take care of himself, I can tell him."

The signal dropped, and the train started without another word being said; but remembering the look on his face, I felt that if they chanced to meet, Joe's danger might be a very real one; and when in a few hours came the dreadful news of Tom's sudden death, almost my first thought was whether he had passed away with his heart still filled with that black jealousy. I got the particulars of the sad event from his fireman that same evening, and found that it was even worse than I thought. It seems that after leaving here the line was clear for them straight through to Keysborough, and by the time they reached Hawkins' crossing they had got up a good speed, and were bowling along merrily; when, as fate would have it, who should they see but that ne'er-do-weel Joe Brown, with his bag of tools on his back, leaning on the gate and talking to Hetty as she gathered flowers in the cottage garden!

The stoker told me that Tom's face was frightful to see; the veins on his forehead swelled as though they would burst, and for the moment he seemed too much choked with rage to speak a word. But he soon found his voice, and broke out into a storm of oaths and curses; and, reckless of all danger, he leaned far out over the side of the engine to look back and shake his fist towards them, though the rise of the bank had already hidden them from sight.

You have guessed how it happened, sir; whilst he in his mad fury was blind to everything, the train dashed under the little wooden foot-bridge, his head struck one of the piers, and he was hurled to the ground. The horrified stoker stopped the train, and went back with one of the guards to pick him up, but they saw at once that the case was a hopeless one, for he was bathed in blood from a terrible cut in the face; indeed the right side of the head, they told me, was regularly beaten in by the force of the blow. They drew up at Keysborough, and the village doctor was fetched, but he pronounced at once that life was extinct.

"No man could have lived for a moment", he said, "after receiving such a stroke as that must have been."

You can imagine how I felt when I heard all this; I don't profess to be better than my neighbours, but it *did* shock me to think of a man's dying in that way with rage in his heart and curses on his lips. Mercifully Hetty Hawkins never heard the whole truth; she had looked up in time to see a black scowl on Tom's face, and she knew that his death must have happened but a few moments afterwards, but she never had the horror of knowing that she, however innocently, was the cause of it. Of course she was grieved to hear of his terrible end, but she had never really returned his love, and I suppose it made no serious impression on her.

It was the topic of conversation among the railway men for a few days; but presently something else took its place. Jack Wilkinson was put in charge of the *Fire Queen*, and Tom Price was almost forgotten. It was whispered at Keysborough that his ghost had been seen once or twice on dark nights, but nobody would admit that he believed the rumour.

It was about the end of May, I think, that this happened; and now I must take my story on to the day of the great accident—the memorable third of July. But before I relate my own experience on that dreadful occasion, I must give you what I myself did not get until the afternoon—an account of what happened in the yard up at the terminus that morning. When Jack Wilkinson came on duty, as he generally did, about an hour before his train was timed to start, his engine, the *Fire Queen*, was not in her usual shed. (Railway men always call their engines 'she' you know, sir, just as sailors do their ships.) He looked all over the yard for her, but she was not to be found anywhere, so he went in search of the turner to make enquiries. He, too, was not in his usual box, but presently Jack saw him among a little crowd of others who were gathered round a man lying on the ground, apparently in a swoon. On reaching the group he found that it was one of the pit-sweepers, a man whom he had known for some time. The sufferer was soon able to speak, but seemed greatly terrified, and when asked what had been the matter, could only say in a trembling voice:

" Tom Price! Tom Price! "

" What's that he says? " cried the turner greatly excited; " has he seen him too? "

Then, in answer to eager enquiries:

" Yes, mates, I swear to you that not half an hour since, when I took the *Fire Queen* into the shed, there I saw Tom Price standing by where I stopped the engine, as plain as ever I saw him in my life; and a frightful object he looked—all covered with blood, and with a great red gash down the right side of his face—so frightful that I jumped right off the other side of the engine, and I have not felt like myself since."

"Yes, yes!" said the shivering pit-sweeper, "that was just how he looked when I saw him; only he came right up to me, so I struck at him with a bar I had in my hand, and it went clear through him as though there was nothing there; and then I went off in a faint, and I don't know what became of him."

No one knew what to make of this story; it was difficult to put it all down to imagination when there were two separate witnesses, and the general opinion was that some trick had been played, though no one could guess how or by whom. When everybody had had their say in the matter, Jack called out:

"Meantime, Mr. Turner, where have you put my engine?"

"You'll find her in the shed, my boy, just where I left her when I saw Tom Price", replied the turner.

"But she's *not* there," said Jack, "and I can't find her anywhere in the yard."

"Perhaps Tom has taken her", said one of the doubters with a laugh.

"Oh, nonsense", replied the turner; "she *must* be there; no one would move her without asking me first."

Off he went to look, and the others after him; but when they got to the shed, sure enough the engine was not there, nor could they find her anywhere, though they searched the whole yard.

"Well; this is queer," said the turner; "she must have run away; let us go and ask the signalman whether he has seen her."

No, he knew nothing of her, he said; certainly some one had taken an engine down the line rather more than half an hour ago, and he had not noticed her come back; but he supposed they were getting up her steam, and thought nothing of it.

"She's gone, and no mistake about it," said the turner; "fetch the superintendent and tell him."

The superintendent was fetched, and at once decided to telegraph to the junction and enquire whether anything had been seen of the missing engine. Back came the answer:

"Yes; single engine passed down the main line at tremendous speed."

"Then she *has* run away, and there is no one on her", said the superintendent; and the men all looked at one another, fearing a terrible accident.

You understand, sir, I knew nothing of all this that I have told you until afterwards; but the morning was so beautiful that I was out and about early to enjoy it, and I was just doing a little in my bit of garden here, when I thought I heard the sound of something coming down the line. I knew there was nothing due for an hour and more, so you may imagine I was surprised, and I thought at first I must be wrong, especially as it did not seem heavy enough for a train.

I stepped out on the platform, and my doubts were soon set at rest, for in a few moments a single engine came into sight round the curve. She was coming along at a very high speed, but as you see this is a steepish incline (a bank, railway men call it) leading up to the station, and that checked her a good deal, so that she swept through not much faster than ordinary. As she approached I recognized her as the *Fire Queen*, but I saw there was only one man on her, and as sure as there is a heaven above us *that man was Tom Price*.

I saw him, sir, I solemnly assure you, as plainly as I see you now, and had no more possibility of making a mistake as to his identity than I have now as to yours. As he passed he turned to look at me, and such a face as I saw then I had never seen before, and I pray God I may never see again. The black scowl of hatred and jealousy was there, and stronger than ever; but with it there was something quite new and much more dreadful—a horrible look of intense, gloating, fiendish triumph that no words can describe. And yet all this terrible, devilish expression was in half the face only, for as he turned in passing I saw that the right side of his head was streaming with blood, and beaten out of all shape and form!

What I felt at the sight of his awful apparition, seen thus in broad daylight on that lovely summer morning, I can never tell you or anyone. How long I stood like one paralysed, staring after it, I do not know; but at last I was roused by the ringing of my telegraph bell. Mechanically I went to the instrument and answered the call from the terminus. The message was to tell me that an engine had run away with no one on her, and that I was to try to throw her off the line to prevent accidents. Then for the first time I saw it all, and it seemed like a great light flashing in upon me and blinding me.

I knew now what that fierce look of joy meant, and my hands shook so I could scarcely send the sad message to tell them that their warning had come too late. I begged them to warn Keysborough, but I felt as I did so that it was useless. I knew that even at that very moment an early market train would be just about leaving Keysborough station; I remembered that the Rector of Keysborough had arranged to take his bible-class out for a picnic among the ruins at Carston, and that, to make the day as long as possible, they were to start by that train; and I knew therefore that pretty Hetty Hawkins and careless Joe Brown, all unconscious of their danger, were in the very track along which that pitiless spectre was hurling fifty tons of iron at seventy miles an hour.

If you read the newspapers at the time you'll know what the result was as well as I do. You don't remember it? Well, it will take but few words to tell you, though it is a dreadful tale. There was the train, crowded as usual with farmers and their wives on their way to the market, and there were the two extra carriages put on behind on purpose for the Rector's party. Everybody was in the highest spirits at the prospect of a glorious day, and the guard was just making ready to start the train, when suddenly, without a minute's warning, the whole bright and busy scene was changed into one of suffering and death.

The heavy engine, coming at that tremendous speed, simply wrecked the train; nearly every carriage was thrown off the metals, and the last three, together with the brake-van, were absolutely reduced to splinters; shattered planks, panels, wheels, axles, door-frames, seats, roofs, were driven about like the chaff from a threshing-floor, and they tell me that the pile of broken wood and twisted iron and mangled corpses was full twenty feet in height.

Many were killed on the spot, and many more—some terribly wounded, some almost unhurt—were imprisoned under that dreadful pile. I suppose only one thing more was wanting to make the horror complete, and in a few moments that thing came, for some of the red-hot ashes had been thrown out of the furnace of the engine in the collision, and the heap of ruins caught fire!

An awful sight it must have been; thank heaven I did not see it, though I have dreamt of it often. Station-master, porters, neighbours, all worked like heroes trying to get the victims out; but the wood was dry and the fire spread rapidly, and I fear many a poor creature must have died the worst of all deaths. The shrieks and cries were piteous to hear, until the good old Rector, who was lying entangled in a heap of woodwork, with an arm and shoulder badly broken, called out in his cheery, commanding voice:

"Hush, boys and girls! Let us bear our pain nobly; all who can, join with me."

And he began to sing a well-known children's hymn. I suppose his noble courage and the instinct of obedience to the voice they were used to follow strengthened them, for one and another joined in, till from that burning pile there rose a ringing chorus:

O, we shall happy be,
When from pain and sorrow free,
Lord, we shall dwell with Thee,
Blest, blest for aye.

The band of workers increased every moment, and presently the fire was got under and the heap of wreckage torn down, and all were saved who were not already past saving. Many, as I have said, were killed, and many more were crippled, and a pretty penny the Company had to pay for compensation; but I think no amount of money can make up to a young man or a young woman for the loss of health or strength just as they are starting in life. The brave old Rector was badly burnt, besides his broken arm; but he slowly recovered, and was able to get about a little in a few week's time. Hetty Hawkins by a sort of miracle was almost unhurt, escaping with a scorched hand and arm and a few slight cuts; but Joe Brown must have been killed on the spot, for his body was found at the very bottom of all, crushed by the weight of half the train; so Tom Price had his revenge.

The Board of Directors held a great enquiry into the cause of the accident, and of course they would not believe the story that Tom had been seen. They could make nothing out of it, except that the engine had certainly run away, and that no one connected with the line or sheds could have been on her; so they decided that one of the cleaning-boys must have been playing with her (as they sometimes will do, if they have a chance) before

8

she made steam, and must have left the regulator open. Two boys were discharged on suspicion, but they declared they were innocent, and I believe quite truly; for I saw Tom Price on that engine, I saw the look on his face; and the decision of a hundred Boards could never persuade me out of that.

Besides, the turner and the pit-sweeper saw him; were *they* both deceived too? People have suggested that there was some one else on the engine, and that our imagination made us take it for Tom; but this I deny. I knew him as well as I do you; I saw him as close and as clearly as I see you; what is the use of telling me I took some one else for him? Besides, if the engine was driven by a human being, where was his body? It must have been found among the victims after the accident, whereas the most careful search revealed no sign of any such person. No, sir; as sure as we stand here now, Tom Price came back from the grave to take his revenge, and an awful revenge he had; I would not have the blood on my soul that he has, for all the gold in the world.

That is my story, sir; I hope it has not wearied you; you understand now why I told you that I believe in ghosts.

The above narrative will, I think, be of interest to the student of psychology. It tells its own story, and requires but little comment. A wicked man dies suddenly with an intense ungratified desire for vengeance; that vengeance he proceeds to take at the earliest opportunity, employing a method which would naturally have been suggested by his previous life. Quite possibly the members of the commission were right in their opinion that the regulator was left open by a boy, since it may have been easier for the dead man to influence the boy to do it than to apply force directly to the handle.

A TRIPLE WARNING

It was at the dinner table of one of the highest dignitaries of the Church—a man whose name, were I at liberty to mention it, would command recognition and respect wherever the English language is spoken—that I heard the two stories which I shall next relate. I am aware that to give the name of the narrator would add greatly to the value of the account with many minds, and indeed, I have no reason to suppose that there would be any objection to my mentioning it; but I did not ask permission to do so (having at the time not the slightest idea of ever publishing the tales) and therefore I refrain.

Whether the stories have been given to the public before by any other writer, and if so where and in what form, I cannot say; the distinguished narrator was of opinion that they had become the theme of common talk, and seemed much surprised that no one present had heard them; but since they were entirely new to the forty or fifty persons gathered round that table, and since I myself have never seen them in print, though I have read most of the extant collections of such stories, I run the risk of repeating what may, perhaps, be to some people an oft-told tale. For the sake of clearness I shall in each case call the chief actor in the story ' the bishop ', though of course, in the first of the cases related, his episcopal honours were far in the future,

The first of his ghostly experiences occurred while ' the bishop ' was still at college. It seems that one night he had retired to bed somewhat earlier than usual, having locked the outer door of his sitting-room, but leaving that between the latter apart-ment and his bed-room standing open. In the sitting-room a large fire was blazing brightly, flood-ing the place with its cheerful light, and rendering every object almost as distinctly visible as at noon-day. It was half-past ten, and the bishop had just laid himself down in blissful expectation of long and uninterruped sleep, when he saw the figure of his father standing in the doorway between the two rooms in the full glare of the light. Surprise held him motionless for a few seconds; he even thinks that he must have watched the play of the firelight upon the sad, earnest face for a whole minute, before the figure raised its hand and beckoned him to come. This dissolved the spell which seemed to hold him in its grasp, and he sprang from the bed and rushed towards the door, but before he could reach it the figure had vanished!

Startled beyond expression, he searched both sitting-room and bed-room thoroughly, and easily convinced himself that he was entirely alone; there was nowhere for an intruder to hide, and the outer door was securely locked as he had left it. Besides, the figure had been distinctly and unmistakably that of his father, looking—except for the intense yearning expressed in his face—exactly as when he had last seen him only a few weeks before; and he was quite convinced that no college joker could have deceived him on this point. He was at last forced to conclude that he must have been the victim of an illusion, hard though it was to bring himself to such an opinion, when he recollected the natural appearance of the figure and the play of the firelight on its face; so he once again composed himself to rest.

The shock, however, had banished sleep for the time, and he lay watching the flickering shadows on the wall for more than an hour before he felt himself sinking again into unconsciousness. Whether he had actually fallen into a doze, or was only on the point of doing so, he was unable to say; but he was suddenly startled into complete wakefulness by the re-appearance of the figure in the doorway, with the same intense expression on its face, and beckoning to him, if possible, even more earnestly than before. Determined that this time, at least, it should not elude him, he sprang with one bound from his bed to the door, and clutched violently at the apparition; but he was again doomed to disappointment; the appearance seemed exactly the same even when he was within a yard of it, yet his outstretched hands grasped only the empty air, and once more the strictest search only confirmed what was already certain—that it was utterly impossible for any bodily presence to have either escaped from the rooms or concealed itself in them.

Like most young men, he had been more or less sceptical upon the subject of apparitions, and, though seriously startled by what he had seen, he endeavoured to reason himself into the belief that it was due to a mere trick of the imagination, arising perhaps from some unsuspected bodily ailment. After bathing his forehead with cold water he therefore retired to rest once more, firmly resolved not to allow his mind to dwell upon what he considered the dream of a distempered brain. As he lay down, the various college clocks chimed midnight, and, with visions of early chapel in his mind, he made the most strenuous efforts to obtain the sleep of which he felt so much need.

At last he was successful, but it seemed to him that he could have been but a few moments unconscious when he awoke with a start, with that feeling of causeless terror at his heart which so often overcomes persons of highly nervous organization when suddenly roused from deep slumber. The fire in the sitting-room had burnt low, and instead of the cheerful dancing light he had seen as he fell asleep, there was now only a dull red glow upon wall and ceiling; but there in the doorway, clearly defined in the midst of that glow, stood his father's figure once more! This time, however, there was a distinct difference in both its expression and its action; instead of the intense yearning which had been so clearly visible before, there was a look of deep though resigned regret, and the raised hand no longer eagerly beckoned him to approach, but slowly and sorrowfully waved him back as he fixed his horror-stricken gaze upon the vision. Instead, too, of vanishing instantly, as before, its outlines became indistinct and it seemed to fade gradually away into the dull red glow upon the wall.

Only upon its disappearance did our young friend recover the power of motion, and his first act was to draw forth his watch and look at the time. It was ten minutes to two—far too early either to arouse any one else or to obtain any sort of conveyance for his homeward journey—for home he at once resolved to go. His father, the rector of a distant country parish, had been perfectly well when he left him a few weeks before, nor had he since heard anything to alarm him in any way;

but, profoundly impressed as he was by the recurrence of the vision, and convinced at last that there was in the matter something of what is usually called the supernatural, he felt that it would be impossible for him to rest until he had satisfied himself by occular demonstration that his father was alive and well. He made no further attempt to sleep, and at the very earliest moment when he thought such an application possible, he sought an interview with the head of his college, explained his fears to him, and set out for home without delay.

The day of rapid travel somewhat weakened the impression that the events of the night had produced upon him, and when, as the shades of evening were beginning to fall, he drove up the well-known lanc leading to the rectory, it was scarcely more than a latent uneasiness which clouded his pleasant anticipations of the astonished greeting of the home circle. It gave him a sudden shock, on coming within sight of the house, to see that all the blinds were drawn closely down; true, it was already growing dusk, but he knew that his father loved the twilight hour, and would never admit candles until they were absolutely necessary; and a nervous apprehension of he hardly knew what, overpowered him so completely that for some moments he was unable to knock at the door. When at last he summoned courage to do so it was opened by the butler—one who had served in the family for many years— whom he had known since childhood; but the first glimpse of this old retainer's face revived in a moment all his worst apprehensions.

"Ah! sir," said the man, "you are too late! if you could only have come last night! Yes," (in answer to his horrified enquiries) "yes, the master is gone; and almost the only words he spoke after he was taken ill were to say how he longed to see you. It was ten o'clock last night when the fit took him, and half an hour afterwards, as soon as he was able to speak, the first thing he said was:

"'Send for my son; I must see my son once more.'

"We told him that a messenger should be sent with the first dawn of day, but he scarcely seemed to hear us, for he had fallen back into a kind of trance. Then at a quarter to twelve he roused up for a few moments, but all he said was;

"'How I wish my son were here!'

"And again just the moment before he died— ten minutes to two it was—he opened his eyes and seemed to know us all, though he was too weak to say much; but he just whispered:

"'I am going; I should like to have spoken to my dear son once more, but I shall not live to see him now.'

" And then he passed away so peacefully, it seemed as though he had but fallen asleep."

Such was the bishop's first experience of life on the super-physical plane—one of a class by no means uncommon, though perhaps an unusually perfect and striking example of its kind. At any rate it is not difficult to believe the remark of the narrator, that it produced on him an impression which time was powerless to obliterate—an impression which coloured his whole after-life.

How many there are among us who have been profoundly affected—whose entire characters even have been changed—by one short glimpse of that world which is ever close around us, though commonly veiled from our eyes! Few people care to speak of such things in this blind and sceptical age, but anyone who takes the trouble to make quiet and earnest enquiries among his friends will be surprised to discover how much more common than he supposed such experiences are.

THE CONCEALED CONFESSION

THE second story which the bishop related to us was of a different character, and its events took place at a much later period of his life, when he was already in charge of a diocese. It appears that on the day on which its events occurred he had accepted an invitation to dinner at a certain country-house in one of the midland counties. Happening to arrive somewhat earlier than usual, he found, on being shown into the drawing-room, that the hostess was not yet down, the only occupant of the room being a Roman Catholic priest, a complete stranger to him, who was seated upon a sofa intently reading a large book. As the bishop entered the priest raised his eyes, made him a courteous but silent bow, and again resumed his reading. He was a strongly built, active-looking man—apparently rather a muscular Christian; but there was in his face an expression of weariness and anxiety that attracted the bishop's attention, and he wondered much within himself who he could be, and how he came to be invited to that house. Soon other guests appeared, and the hostess came down so full of apologies for not being in readiness to receive her principal guest on his arrival, that the questions he had intended to ask about the stranger-priest were forgotten for the time. When seated next to his hostess at the dinner-table, however, they recurred to his memory, and turning to her he remarked:

"By the way, you did not introduce me to that interesting-looking priest whom I found in the drawing-room; who is he?"

Then, looking along the table, he continued with some surprise:

"He does not seem to have come in to dinner."

A very strange look passed over the hostess's face as she said hurriedly, almost in a whisper:

"What, did you actually see him, then?"

"Certainly I did;" replied the bishop; "but I beg your pardon; I fear I have unintentionally mentioned a subject which is unpleasant to you— perhaps intruded upon some family secret. I had no idea but that the priest was a simple guest here, like myself, and his appearance interested me so much that I wished to ask for an introduction; but if you are anxious for some reason that his presence here should be concealed, I need hardly assure you that you may depend upon my silence."

"No, no, my lord," answered the hostess still in a low tone, "you misunderstand me entirely; there is nothing which I wish to conceal, though this is a subject which my husband does not like to have mentioned. I was surprised to hear that the priest had shown himself to you, because until now this has never happened except to a member of our own family. What you saw was no visitor, but an apparition".

" An apparition? " ejaculated the bishop.

" Yes," continued the hostess, " and one whose supernatural character it is impossible to doubt, for during the two years we have lived in this house it has shown itself perhaps a dozen times to my husband and myself under circumstances in which either self-deception or imposition were quite out of the question. Since we cannot explain it, and are well assured that it is due to no natural causes, we have decided not to speak of it to any one. But since you have seen it—my lord, will you do me a favour? "

" Most certainly, if it be within my power ", replied he.

" I have often thought," she resumed, " that if any one could be found who had the courage to address it, we might perhaps be relieved from its presence. I have always feared that some day the children may see it, or that the servants may be terrified and insist upon leaving the house. Can you—will you—make some trivial excuse for going back into the drawing-room for a few minutes, see if the priest be still there, and, if he be, speak to him—adjure him to depart from this house—exorcise him in fact?"

After some hesitation the bishop agreed to make the proposed experiment. His low-toned conversation with the hostess having been apparently unobserved, he excused himself to her in a louder voice for a few moments' absence, and left the room, waving back the servant who would have attended him. It was with a strange thrill of awe that, on entering the drawing-room, he perceived the figure of the priest still seated in the same spot—still diligently perusing his great breviary, if such it was; but with unshaken resolution he walked slowly forward, and stood directly in front of the apparition. As before, the priest greeted him with a courteous inclination of the head, but this time instead of immediately returning to the book his eyes rested, with a look of infinite weariness, and with a kind of suppressed eagerness also, upon the bishop's face. After a moment's pause, the latter said slowly and solemnly:

"In the name of God, who are you and what do you want?"

The apparition closed its book, rose from its seat, stood confronting him, and after a slight hesitation, spoke in a low but clear and measured voice:

" I have never been so adjured before; I will tell you who I am and what I want. As you see, I am a priest of the Catholic Church. Eighty years ago, this house in which we now stand was mine. I was a good rider, and was extremely fond of hunting when opportunity offered; and one day I was just about to start for the neighbouring meet, when a young lady of very high family indeed called upon me for the purpose of making a confession. What she said, of course, I may not repeat, but it affected very closely the honour of one of the noblest houses of England; and it appeared to me of such supreme importance that (there being certain complications in the case) committed the grave indiscretion—the sin even, for it is strictly forbidden by our Church—of making notes of the confession as I heard it.

" When I had absolved and dismissed her, I found that it was only barely possible for me to reach the rendezvous in time, but even in my haste I did not forget the supreme importance of guarding carefully my notes of the terrible secret just committed to me. For purposes which I need not now detail, I had had a few bricks loosened in the wall of one of the lower passages of this house and a small recess made —just the place, I thought, in which my notes would be perfectly safe from any conceivable accident until my return, when I intended to master the intricacies of the case at my leisure and then at once destroy the dangerous paper. Meantime I hurriedly shut it between the leaves of the book I had held in my hand, ran downstairs, thrust the book into the recess, replaced the bricks, sprang upon my horse, and rode off at full speed.

"That day in the hunting-field I was thrown from my horse and killed on the spot; and ever since it has been my dreary fate to haunt this earthly home of mine and try to avert the consequences of my sin —try to guard from any possibility of discovery the fatal notes which I so rashly and wrongly made. Never until now has any human being dared to speak to me boldly as you have done; never until now has there seemed aught of help for me or hope of deliverance from this weary task; but now—will you save me? if I show you where my book is hidden, will you swear by all that you hold most sacred to destroy the paper that it contains without reading it—without letting any human eye see even one word of its contents? Will you pledge your word to do this?"

"I pledge my word to obey your wish to the letter", said the bishop with solemnity.

The gaze of the priest's eyes was so intense that they seemed to pierce his very soul, but apparently the result of the scrutiny was satisfactory, for the phantom turned away with a deep sigh of relief, saying:

9

"Then follow me."

With a strange sense of unreality the bishop found himself following the apparition down the broad staircase to the ground floor, and then down a narrower one of stone that seemed to lead to some cellars or vaults. Suddenly the priest stopped and turned towards him.

"This is the place," he said, placing his hand on the wall; "remove this plaster, loosen the bricks, and you will find behind them the recess of which I spoke. Mark the spot well, and—remember your promise."

Following the pointing hand and the apparent wish of the spectre, the bishop closely examined the wall at the spot indicated, and then turned to the priest to ask another question; but to his intense astonishment there was no one there—he was absolutely alone in the dimly-lighted passage! Perhaps he ought to have been prepared for this sudden disappearance, but it startled him more than he cared to admit even to himself. He retained sufficient presence of mind to draw a penknife from his pocket and make a scratch upon the wall, and also to leave the knife itself at the foot of the wall to guide him to the spot; then he hurried up the stairs, and presented himself, still breathless with surprise, in the dining-room.

His prolonged absence had caused some comment, and now his agitated appearance excited general attention. Unable for the moment to speak coherently, his only answer to the earnest questions of his host was a sign which referred him to the hostess for explanation. With some hesitation she confessed the errand upon which her request had despatched his lordship, and as may easily be imagined, intense interest and excitement were at once created. As soon as the bishop had recovered his voice, he found himself compelled to relate the story before the entire party, concealment being now out of the question.

Celebrated as was his eloquence, it is probable that no speech he ever made was followed with closer attention than this; and at its conclusion there was no voice to oppose the unanimous demand that a mason be at once sent for to break down the wall and search for confirmation of this weird yet dramatically circumstantial tale. After a short delay the man arrived, and the whole company trooped eagerly downstairs under the bishop's guidance to watch the result of his labours. He could hardly repress a shudder as he found himself once more in the passage where his ghostly companion had vanished so unceremoniously; but he indicated the exact spot which had been pointed out to him, and the mason began to work upon it forthwith.

" The plaster seems very hard and firm ", remarked some one.

"Yes," replied the host, "it is of excellent quality, and comparatively new; these vaults had been long disused, I am told, until my predecessor had the old brick-work repaired and plastered over only a few years ago."

By this time the mason had succeeded in breaking away the plaster and loosening a brick or two at the point indicated, and though perhaps no one was actually surprised, yet there was a very perceptible stir of excitement among the guests when he announced the existence of a cupboard or cavity about two feet square and eighteen inches deep in the thickness of the wall. The host pressed forward to look in, but instantly recollecting himself, drew back and made way for the bishop, saying:

"I was forgetting your promise for the moment; to you alone belongs the right of the first investigation here."

Pale, but collected, the bishop stepped up to the cavity, and after one glance put in his hand and drew forth a heavily bound, old-fashioned book, thickly covered with dust or mould. A thrill ran through the assembled guests at the sight, but no words broke the silence of awe-stricken expectation while he reverently opened the volume, and turning over a few leaves, drew from between the pages a piece of writing paper, yellow with age, on which were some irregular, hastily-written lines. As soon as he was certain that he had found what he sought, he averted his eyes from it, and, the others falling back to make way for him, bore it carefully up the stairs and into the nearest room and cast it reverently into the fire burning on the hearth, almost as though he were laying a sacred offering upon some ancient Zoroastrian altar.

Until the last scrap of the mysteriously found document was reduced to cinder, no one spoke; and even then, though a few disjointed exclamations of "Marvellous! wonderful indeed! who could have believed it?" broke forth, the majority were far too deeply impressed for words. The bishop felt that none who were present on that occasion could ever forget its lessons—he himself least of all, and indeed he could never tell the story, even after years had passed, without the profoundest emotion. The figure of the priest, he added, was never seen again in the house where he had so long guarded his guilty secret.

We can readily realize what that priest's feelings must have been when the accident threw him suddenly out of his physical body, and he knew that he would be unable to repair the consequences of his indiscretion. An added difficulty was that the very nature of his secret was such that there was scarcely anyone to whom he could trust it; and he must have had perpetual anxiety lest it should be discovered by the wrong person, while he was waiting for the right one to whom he could entrust its destruction.

This again, like the previous story, is an example of a well-attested and not infrequent class of phenomena, and is specially remarkable only from the high position of the principal actor, and, perhaps, for a certain perfection of detail—an artistic finish, as it were—which, if this account were a fiction, would be supposed to do credit to the conceptive powers of the writer. The person from whom, and the circumstances under which, I heard it, precluded, however, the slightest possibility of its having acquired a romantic tinge, as might be the case had it passed through many hands instead of coming direct from the fountain head; and for my part I can only say that I have been, as ever, scrupulously exact in its reproduction, using in many cases, I believe, even the exact words in which it was originally told.

JAGANNATH

A TALE OF HIDDEN INDIA

"You Europeans know nothing of Jagannath," said my friend Mr. T. Subba Rao, as we lay in our long chairs on the flat roof at Adyar, in the glorious tropical moonlight.

"Your travellers and missionaries have allowed themselves to be deceived by the statements of the priests and devotees of that horrible worship—statements which were doubtless intentionally misleading. Why, I have actually seen in one of your books the remark that the cult in question is merely a variety of that of Vishnu! Perhaps long ago it was, but for centuries it has been simply the worship of an earth-spirit of the most bloodthirsty description.

"I will tell you the true story of the matter. There will be no harm in my doing so, for if you repeat it no one will believe you—unless, indeed, it be a man who already knows all about it, and *he* will at once deny its truth, lest the ghastly horror of it should come to the knowledge of the

Government, from which it has always been (and always will be) hidden with such elaborate care. Wildly incredible as it may seem to the Occidental unbeliever, it is nevertheless terribly true, as I have good cause to know.

"To make my story intelligible I must begin at the beginning. Long ago—long before what you acknowledge as history begins—a mighty convulsion in a far-distant continent drove away from their home some of the priests of the old Nature-religion, and after weary wandering they at last settled down at the spot now called Jagannath. Their power over the elements, which for many years they used only for good, gained them respect and fear among the inhabitants; but as the ages passed on their successors degenerated into utter selfishness, and their college became a mere school of evil magic.

"At last a leader, more unscrupulous or more daring than his predecessors, succeeded in invoking and partially subjugating a malignant earth-spirit of terrible power, by whose assistance he committed atrocities so abominable that even his abandoned followers rose against him and assassinated him. But though they could slay him they could not dismiss the demon he had raised, and it carried destruction far and wide throughout the district, so that the affrighted priests knew not what to do.

"Eventually they bethought them of applying for aid to a celebrated magician of the north, whose power was used always for purer and nobler purposes than theirs had been. After much persuasion he consented, not for their sake but for that of the helpless populace around, to do what was now possible to restrain the evil influence so recklessly invoked. But bad was the best that could be done; for strange as it may appear to your ideas, the laws of magic require that strict justice shall be shown even to such an entity as this. All that was found possible was to limit the evil—so to arrange matters that the priests might make a kind of agreement with the fiend that, instead of indulging in promiscuous destruction, it should be satisfied with taking such lives as were voluntarily yielded to it; and all through the centuries since, the strange wild covenant then made has been duly fulfilled.

"The terms of the treaty will be unfolded as I relate to you what it is that really happens at each of the great septennial festivals which have ever since been regularly held in honour of the so-called god. First comes what is known as 'The Day of the Wood'. On a certain morning a vast but silent crowd assembles before daybreak on the seashore. On the beach the priests of the temple are grouped round their chief; and a little in advance of them, nearest to the water, stand two doomed men—the priest and the carpenter—doomed by the terms of that terrible compact.

"For, when first that unholy agreement was made, seven families of the hereditary priesthood and seven families of carpenters (you know that trades also are hereditary with us) vowed in return for a promise of temporal prosperity—which has always been honourably kept—to devote, each in turn, a representative to the service of the deity at the septennial festivals. So the two who have been chosen for the dread honour on this occasion stand apart, regarded with awe as already half-belonging to the realms of the supernatural.

"As the sun rises from the ocean all eyes are eagerly strained towards the eastern horizon, and a proud man is he who first catches sight of a tiny black speck far out at sea drawing steadily nearer and nearer to the awe-stricken crowd on shore. When the object approaches it is seen to consist of three logs of wood, floating side by side, though not fastened together—moving with undeviating course, though without any apparent motive power. A trick of the priests, you think? You would not say so if you had seen it, my friend! Possibly your boasted western science might succeed in imitating the phenomenon by the aid of elaborate and costly machinery; but how could it be done by these priests who know nothing of such means, and are besides in the midst of a multitude who watch their every movement?

"Be that as it may, the logs at last reach the shore, and are reverently lifted by the priests and borne away to a hut in the temple enclosure, where the chosen carpenter is to do his work. Eagerly he sets about his task, which is to carve from these mysterious logs three images in exact imitation of those already standing in the innermost shrine of the temple; and day after day he labours on with an ardent devotion to his object, which leaves him hardly time for food or sleep. First the two attendant figures or supporters are finished; then he commences upon the central image—the representation of the deity himself. And the neighbours tell with bated breath how at this period of his arduous labour he is always encouraged by the apparition of the 'god' himself—an apparition visible to him only, but thenceforward never absent from his consciousness, whether waking or sleeping, and ever drawing steadily nearer and nearer to him as his work approaches completion.

"At last the image is finished, and the workman who has spent so much loving care and devoted energy upon it lies down beside it, and resigns himself altogether to the dread apparition. Nearer and nearer it comes, and more and more rapid becomes the action of that intense magnetic attraction that is draining the man's life away. The effect of imagination, you say? Perhaps; but the result is the same; in no case has the carpenter survived the accomplishment of his task by as much as twelve hours.

"Almost immediately after this comes 'The Day of Procession', the culminating point of the festival; and it is on this occasion that the doomed priest performs his share of the terrible contract. Early on the day appointed, in the presence of an immense gathering, the new images are reverently borne by the priests into the innermost sanctuary, and there laid on the ground before the platform on which their three predecessors have stood for the last seven years. All but the chosen priest then retire from the sanctuary, and the great doors which shut it off from the body of the temple are closed, leaving the especial minister of the 'god alone to perform the mystic rites which no human eye but his may see.

"Exactly what takes place within those closed doors no one has ever known—no one will ever know; for none of those who alone could tell ever live long enough to lift the veil from the awful mystery. The priests lie prostrate in adoration outside the doors as a guard of honour to prevent any possibility of disturbance; but their office is a sinecure, for no native of India could be bribed to enter that sanctuary during the Hour of Silence, even by all the fabled jewels of Golconda. The vast crowd in the body of the temple remains wrapped in the most profound stillness until the hour is over, when the high priest rises from the ground and with reverent awe opens the great doors once more.

"Not the faintest sound has reached the listening ears without, but the heavy images have changed places; the new ones are in position on the platform, while the older ones are cast aside on the ground, and beside them lies the priest, speechless—dying. It is recorded that he expires always within a few minutes of the opening of the doors, and never yet has any victim been able to indicate by word or sign the nature of the ordeal through which he has passed.

"This much is known—that the carpenter is instructed when making the idols to drill a long cylindrical hole of a certain given diameter in each figure, roughly corresponding in location to the spinal column in a human being, and tradition whispers that one of the duties of the doomed priest is to remove. *something*—something that none may see and live—from this strange receptacle in the old images to a corresponding place in the new ones. For the rest the will of the deity is said to impress upon the mind of its devoted servant the ceremonial which has to be carried out.

" Meanwhile, outside the temple, all has been prepared for the great procession, and the huge wooden car of the deity has been dragged to the door. This vehicle is a curious one, and rather difficult to describe without the aid of a picture or a model. The lower part of it may be said to resemble an immense oblong chest richly carved round the sides with figures of the Gods, each in its separate shrine, deeply recessed and protected by beautifully moulded pillars; and upon this as a platform, or pedestal, stands a colossal statue of a rampant lion, bearing on its back a sort of canopied pulpit.

" When the hour arrives the chief priest, bending low before the new image, hangs garlands of flowers round its neck in the usual Hindu fashion, and fastens round its waist a magnificently jewelled belt. And now by the strength which it has absorbed from its victims, this demon favours its faithful votaries with a marvellous exhibition of its uncanny powers. A piece of thin silk cord about twenty feet long is passed through the idol's belt, and its ends are held by two priests, who are thus some ten feet in advance of the image, though not directly in its path. The central passage of the temple is cleared, and the two priests gently pull the cord. On receiving this signal the heavy wooden idol *advances by a series of bounds* down the path left for it, the priests retiring before it, and, apparently, initiating each leap by the same gentle pull. Quite impossible, you say? or if actually done, then a trick of the priests. Think so, if you will; but *how* is it done? The pull given by the priests is a mere movement of the finger and thumb, scarcely strong enough even to tighten the cord, and it is certain that no other mechanical force is employed.

"But a still greater wonder is to come. When the idol, in the manner described, has reached the door where its car awaits it, the two priests climb upon the platform, still holding the ends of their line. At their next pull the image springs upon the platform beside them, and then, without waiting for any further guidance, makes another leap into its pulpit, and turns itself half round so as to face the front of the car! Incredible, is it? Yet there are thousands who can bear testimony to it. And after all, *why* incredible? If a heavy table can jump about in the West, as some of your greatest scientists have seen that it can, why may not a heavy image do the same in the East? 'There are more things in heaven and earth than are dreamt of in your philosophy', and one fact is worth many theories.

"After this astonishing display of power, the great procession starts and the image is carried in triumph about the town, offerings of all kinds being thrown upon the car as it moves along, while t he many little bells which are hung about it tinkle joyously, and the thronging multitudes shout in adoration. It was during this progress that devotees used sometimes to throw themselves under the wheels of the car, holding it an honour to yield up the life so crushed out of them as a willing sacrifice to their sanguinary deity. Your Government thinks it has put an end to all that; but devotion is not to be wiped out by an edict, and perhaps, in one way or another, Jagannath gains about as many lives as he ever did. The covenant which binds him not to slay promiscuously in no way precludes him from accepting life voluntarily offered to him, or even from endeavouring to influence weak-minded worshippers to immolate themselves at his shrine, and no doubt he does so whenever it is possible.

"A weird and terrible story, is it not? But many strange things happen in remote corners of India which are entirely unsuspected by the ruling race—things which would be to them quite as inconceivable as is this studiously accurate account of the festival of Jagannath.

THE BARON'S ROOM

MADAME HELENA PETROVNA BLAVATSKY was a many-sided genius—the most remarkable personality I have ever met. Her followers naturally think of her as the great occult teacher to whom we all owe so much, but to us who had the privilege of knowing her in the flesh she is very much more than that, and we have in our minds pictures of her as filling many and various parts. She was, for example, a weirdly brilliant performer on the piano on the very rare occasions when she chose to exhibit that talent. Though she hated conventionality, and often went out of her way quite unnecessarily to outrage it, (or so we used to think in those days), I have never seen anyone who could better play the part of the great aristocrat when she chose to do so. On any and all subjects she was an exceptionally brilliant conversationalist; but that which more than all others she made her own was the domain of the occult. All her narrations were witty and dramatic, but she was at her best when telling a ghost-story.

I shall never forget the evenings we used to spend in listening to her on the deck of the s.s. *Navarino,* when I was travelling with her from Egypt to India in the year 1884. The missionary element was strong in the motley gathering of our fellow passengers, and some of its representatives were of the coarsely ignorant and blatantly aggressive type which was perhaps commoner then than now. Passages of arms were frequent, and to us intensely amusing, for Madame Blavatsky knew the Christian scriptures and the Christian faith very much better than these self-appointed exponents of them. But even the crossest of the missionaries had to succumb to her charm when she began to tell ghost-stories on the deck after dinner in the evenings. She held her audience spell-bound, she played on them as on an instrument and made their hair rise at pleasure, and I have often noticed how careful they were to go about in couples after one of her stories, and to avoid being alone even for a moment!

Under these circumstances we heard " The Cave of the Echoes ", " The Bewitched Life ", and other legends which all who will may read in her *Nightmare Tales*. One striking tale I remember, which does not appear in that collection. If I could hope to tell it as she told it, my readers might perhaps share something of the feeling with which we heard it; but I know that cannot be. I told it once, as well as I could, to a friend who is a well-known novelist; she did her best with it, altering it in various particulars to make it more effective and dramatic, and adding many picturesque touches; but even that best could not reproduce the magical charm with which Madame Blavatsky's narration invested it. I cannot hope to do even as well as the novelist; but anyhow I shall try, and I shall adhere as closely as possible to my recollection of the original form as Madame Blavatsky gave it.

Two young men (let us call them Charles and Henri) were on a walking tour in one of the most picturesquely beautiful parts of the pleasant land of France. One day, as evening was drawing on, they found themselves approaching a pretty little town which lies in a secluded valley, its inns, its shops and its smaller houses clustering round a little stream, while the larger dwellings of the more important inhabitants are situated on the gentle slopes of the surrounding hills. The two friends expected to pass the night at the principal inn of the place, and one of them, Monsieur Charles, had an acquaintance living on the outskirts of the town upon whom he wished to call.

Just as the road began to slope down into the village, they came in sight of a specially picturesque old house, almost covered with ivy and creepers. It stood back some little distance from the road, and both the house itself and its extensive grounds bore an air of neglect which showed quite clearly that it was unoccupied, and indeed, that it must have been so for a long series of years. The friends were much struck by its appearance and the beauty of its situation, and Henri, who was an enthusiastic collector of old-fashioned furniture, began at once to speculate upon the treasures which might lie concealed there. Since the place was so obviously unoccupied, it was natural that the idea should suggest itself that possibly they might persuade its custodian to let them look over it; so they directed their steps towards a little lodge which, though it partook of the general air of neglect and was almost overgrown with luxurious vegetation, was still evidently inhabited.

In answer to their knock a very old man came to the door. They asked for permission to look through the house, but the old man told them with polite regrets that it was not allowed. They fell into conversation with this old care-taker, who indeed had the air of one who leads a lonely life, and is glad of an opportunity to talk with his fellow-men. Henri at once enquired about the furniture, and when he heard that it was old—very old—and that everything remained untouched, precisely as it had been many years ago when the house was inhabited, he was seized with an irresistible desire to see it, and he intimated to the old man, as delicately as possible, that he was prepared to offer a substantial present for the privilege. But the old man only replied:

"No, monsieur, I am sorry, but it is impossible; I should be glad enough to avail myself of your generosity, for I am a poor man, as you see, and times are hard with me. But it is quite impossible."

"But, after all", said Henri, "why impossible? The place has evidently been unoccupied for years; this is a lonely road; no one is passing; no one will ever know; why should you not gratify us by allowing us to see the rooms, and at the same time profit yourself?"

"Ah, monsieur, I dare not", said the old man. "It is not because of the owner or the agent; as you say, they would never know. It is far more than that, far worse than that! Indeed, I dare not do it."

Scenting a mystery here, the friends pressed the old man to reveal his real reason, and at last with much difficulty and persuasion they drew from him the admission that the house bore an evil reputation, that terrible things had happened there, and that for twenty years at least no one had entered it except when at long intervals the agent came down and made some sort of inspection of it. If Henri was an enthusiast for old furniture, he was even more deeply interested in matters psychical. At once he suspected here an interesting story, so he enquired:

"You say the house bears a bad reputation. Do you mean that it is said to be haunted?"

"Alas! yes, monsieur," replied the old man, "but it is no mere rumour; it is terribly true."

Of course after this our friends would not be satisfied until they had heard the whole story, though they had much difficulty in extracting it from the old man, who seemed very reluctant to speak of it, and crossed himself repeatedly while telling the tale. It was simple enough; the last owner had been a man of dark and evil life—a man who had the reputation of indulging in orgies of wild debauchery, of being a monster of cruelty, selfishness and lust. The old man knew no details; but in some way or other, the Baron's sins had found him out, and his affairs came to some sort of terrible crisis, from which he had escaped (or thought he had escaped) by suicide. He had come down quite unexpectedly from Paris one evening, and the next morning he was found sitting in his great chair with his throat cut.

After this there had been a terrible exposure of some sort, the old man said, and all kinds of dreadful stories had come out. He knew little of their nature; it was all many years ago, and he had never really understood it. There was some litigation, he thought, and all the riches of the family were somehow swallowed up, and the house passed into the hands of a distant branch of the family. It was, he said, many years after the Baron's death before the legal business was settled, and the new owner came into possession. Even then the house was not touched in any way; it was to be left for the inspection of the new master, but an army of gardeners was sent in, and the grounds were all put into order. The new master came down with his wife and some servants, but after one night in the house they returned to Paris, declaring that nothing would induce them to enter the place again.

"What happened to them," said Henri eagerly; "what did they see?"

"That I do not know, monsieur," replied the old man; "there were many stories, but I never really knew which was true. Then the owners tried to let the house. Twice tenants came, but neither of them stopped more than the one night. In the second case there was a scandal; a lady in the family was so terrified that she fell into a series of fits. They tell me that she went mad afterwards and died; and since then no further effort has been made to let the place. But on four occasions strangers have arrived with a note from the owner, giving them permission to sleep in the house, and in every case frightful evil has followed. One of them cut his throat, like Monsieur le Baron; another was found dead in a fit, and the other two were driven mad by terror. So the reputation of the place has grown worse and worse."

"Now my good friend, see here", said Henri, "and pay particular attention to what I am going to say. I told you that I was interested in old furniture, and I was willing to give you a napoleon to let me see what you had in the château. But I am a hundred times more interested in haunted houses, and after what you have told me I positively must and will spend a night in this one, and I will give you a hundred francs if you will let me do so."

"Indeed, sir," replied the old man, "I do assure you that it is quite impossible; you would die without doubt, and I should be your murderer. Indeed, I wish I could, but it is useless to ask me."

But all this protestation only made Henri more determined, and he steadily increased his offer, assuring the old man that whatever might happen he should be held entirely guiltless, and that if he preferred it, he might shut himself up in his own cottage and have no part whatever in the affair beyond leaving open the door. The care-taker was in an agony of indecision. The heavy bribe offered was unquestionably a great consideration to him, and still more his kindly French courtesy could not bear to disappoint the persuasive stranger, who had so evidently set his heart upon trying this experiment. Yet his superstitious fear was stronger than his greed, and it took the best part of an hour's talk to win from him a reluctant and tearful consent.

He agreed to take them over the house now in the daylight, and to point out to them the haunted room of Monsieur le Baron; and when they came again in the darkness of night, since come they must, (and he wrung his hands in despair) he would give them the key, yes, if they would call for it at his little gate-house, but on no account must they expect him then to come outside his own door, or go any nearer to the haunted building. And even so, over and over again, he asserted that he washed his hands of all responsibility, that their doom was certain, and he could but commend their souls to God.

They spoke heartily to him, they clapped him on the shoulder, they assured him that to-morrow morning he should drink a bottle of wine with them, and laugh over all his presentiments; but nothing that they could say moved him in the least from his melancholy certainty of their immediate destruction. He showed them over the house, in which Henri went into raptures over splendid specimens of wonderful old furniture; he directed their attention to the Baron's portrait in the drawing-room; he pointed out to them the long room on the ground floor which had been the Baron's special study, and indicated to them the identical arm-chair in which he had committed suicide. Before they left they pressed upon him the money which they had promised him; yet, badly as he obviously needed it, he took it with manifest reluctance, saying:

"Messieurs, this is a fortune for me, and yet I feel as though I could not take it, for I believe that it is the price of your lives; and who knows but that it may be the price of your immortal souls as well? Monsieur le Baron was an evil man, and who knows what happens to his victims?"

So they left him, impressed in spite of themselves by his invincible gloom and his despairful attitude, even though they smiled to themselves at it while they talked over the adventure that lay before them. So they went their way into the charming little town and sat themselves down to such refreshment as the bright little inn could give them. They had covenanted to be back at the haunted house at half-past ten, and now it was hardly six.

Charles, as we have said, had some friends in the neighbourhood whom he wished to visit; he had pointed out their house to Henri as they descended the hill into the town. These friends were unknown to Henri, and as he had some urgent letters to write he excused himself from accompanying Charles on his visit. Presently the latter reappeared, bearing a most cordial invitation to dinner from his friends for both the tourists; but Henri had not finished his letters, so he begged Charles to go alone and to make his excuses, but promised to call for him at his friends' house at half-past ten, since that house lay in the general direction of the haunted chateau, and would be but little out of his way as he walked there from the hotel. This understood, Charles started off once more to his friends', while Henri ordered for himself a little dinner at the hotel, and sat down again to his writing.

In due course of time he had his dinner and finished his letters. Having posted them, he started a few minutes before half-past ten for the house which Charles had pointed out to him. While he had been writing his thoughts were fully occupied with his work, but now that he was free from that, the adventure upon which he was about to embark loomed large on his horizon, and he could not but admit to himself that on the whole it looked distinctly less pleasant and heroic, now that night had fallen, than it had done in the warm glow of the summer afternoon.

He was even conscious of a half-formed desire to escape from it all and go snugly to bed in that clean little hotel; but he put away these craven thoughts from him, asking himself how he could miss so splendid an opportunity, and still more how he could be so selfish as to think of disappointing Charles, who in his quieter way was just as eager for the adventure as he had previously been himself. He owned to himself quite cynically that he felt distinctly nervous, and that if he were there alone, he should instantly abandon the undertaking; but he thought that with the encouragement and support of his more phlegmatic friend's presence, he might contrive to get through the affair creditably. But his thoughts *would* return uncomfortably to the grim fate of those four predecessors, and he wondered whether any of them had felt as nervous as he did.

Presently he arrived at the appointed house, and there, in the shadow of a little porch at the top of the steps which led up to the front door, he saw Charles already expecting him—evidently punctual to the minute and eager to waste no time, since instead of waiting to be called for, he had already finished his leave-taking and shut the door behind him. Henri called out a hearty word of greeting to him, but it seemed to him that Charles scarcely answered him, as he descended the steps. The night was not a very dark one, but still he could not see his friend's face at all clearly when he tried to peer into it. Though he could see so little, it seemed to him that Charles was hardly himself; he appeared to be *distrait*, preoccupied, almost sullen in the short answers which he gave to his friend's questions.

After a few unavailing attempts to draw him into cheery conversation, Henri tactfully let him alone, making only now and then some casual remark on indifferent subjects, which did not call for reply. He thought that perhaps some unfortunate *contretemps* at his friend's house had annoyed Charles, or perhaps that he had heard some bad news. But he did not ask further what was the matter, feeling sure that his friend would confide in him in his own good time. His own sensations, meantime, were far from pleasant. His nervousness seemed to be increasing, and he felt as though something was steadily, slowly but relentlessly sucking away his strength, his courage, his very life. Never had he been so strangely, so uncomfortably affected before.

Thus their walk to the haunted house was a somewhat silent one. When they knocked at the door of the old care-taker's cottage, he met them with fresh outbursts of protestations and lamentations, telling them that the more he thought over this project of theirs the more he felt that he could not possibly be a party to it. He even went the length of offering to return their money to them, declaring that he could not reconcile it to his conscience to accept it. Henri, however pressed it upon him with kindly and cheering words, averring that all would be well, and that when they met safe and sound in the morning, he would even add a trifle extra to the very handsome present that he had already made.

The old care-taker made a dignified protest against this, assuring them that he was already much overpaid, and that if indeed they were so fortunate as to escape with their lives and their reason, it would be sufficient joy to him to see them safe and in good health when the morning dawned. Henri was really moved at the old man's solicitude, and pressed his hand heartily in bidding him good-night. Charles had all this time remained in the background saying practically nothing—nothing at any rate that was not absolutely necessary. Evidently his dark humour had not yet been completely shaken off, and Henri wondered much what could be the cause which in those few short hours had so entirely changed the mood of his friend.

They unlocked the door, they entered the great forsaken house, and, having provided themselves with a dark lantern, they made their way without difficulty to the study of the late Baron. A curious room it was, built out into the garden at one side of the house, as a billiard room sometimes is, suggesting that it had been added at some later period and was no part of the original design. It was a long and narrow room, with many French windows opening down to the floor at each side along its length; but each end of the room was almost entirely occupied by a huge pier-glass. This produced a remarkable effect, for as one looked along the room, it gave the illusion of extending to infinity in both directions, everything in it being repeated again and again in a seemingly endless vista. There was a good deal of furniture of one sort and another, and in each of the four corners a suit of armour was arranged precisely as though there was a figure inside it. In the centre of the room was a large and well-appointed writing-table, in front of which stood the Baron's chair—the chair in which he had committed suicide.

Our friends had bargained that the old man should leave a lamp ready trimmed for them, and they soon had it alight. So large a room, however, would have needed twenty lamps to make it really cheerful, and the far-away corners were still suggestively gloomy. A curious and eerie effect was produced by the indefinite reproduction of the light in the great mirrors at each end of the room. The place had the close musty smell which always haunts a room that has long been closed; and altogether Henri was acutely conscious of a sense of discomfort and of a yearning for the comfortable, prosaic, nineteenth-century bedroom at the hotel.

Besides, he was growing weaker and weaker; he felt exactly as a living fly might feel when a spider was slowly sucking away his life-blood, and leaving him a mere empty shell. Clearly it would never do to admit this, so he tried to conceal his qualms by light and easy conversation, and attempted to rally Charles upon his taciturnity and apparent lowness of spirits. He received only the briefest of replies, and it was evident that Charles was still in the same strange mood; indeed, it would seem that if anything he had sunk into it more deeply than ever. Now that Henri could see him clearly in the brilliant light of the lamp, he became still more impressed with the oddity of his friend's appearance and behaviour. It would seem that Charles himself was to some extent conscious of this, and tried to avoid the light. He had thrown himself upon a settee, and for a long time he remained there motionless, answering only in surly monosyllables the sprightly observations of his friend.

After a time, however, this strange inertia was replaced by an equally strange disquiet, for he sprang up suddenly from the settee and began to walk up and down the long room like a wild animal marching up and down his cage. And it seemed to Henri, unless his imagination was playing tricks with him, that this suggestion of a wild beast was more than a mere simile; it was not only the restless marching up and down, but a curious air of repressed ferocity which somehow permeated the usual gentle and pacific bearing of his friend. Henri could not understand his own feelings, and tried to throw them off as ridiculous; but the persistent march up and down got upon his weakened nerves at last to such an extent that he was compelled to beg his friend to desist. The latter seemed scarcely to understand him—at least not until he had repeated his words more than once; and then with a curious, half-impatient exclamation he once more threw himself down upon the settee —no longer, however, to remain lethargic, for it was evident that his restlessness was still upon him, and that he could not retain the same position for more than a few seconds.

All this began to make Henri decidedly uncomfortable; he felt that no ordinary pre-occupation could fully account for this change, and he began to fear that some illness was falling upon his friend. He began also very heartily to wish that he had not been so eager to enter upon this adventure, for, as has already been said, it was upon the presence and upon the assistance of his friend that he had relied to carry it through to a successful conclusion; and now in some strange way this seemed to be failing him. However, the hour of midnight, at which the Baron was supposed to appear, was now rapidly drawing near, and he determined that, as soon as it was decently possible after that witching hour was past, he would get his friend safely back to the hotel and into bed, and if there was not a distinct change for the better by the next morning, he would consult the village doctor.

Meantime Charles's agitation appeared to have become uncontrollable; once more he sprang to his feet and resumed the strange, stealthy and subtly-threatening march backwards and forwards. And now he altogether disregarded his friend's remarks, seeming not even to hear them, but throwing all his energy into that weird and ceaseless promenade. It seemed to Henri, as he watched him, that his very face was changing, and inapposite reminiscences came to his mind of the way in which at a spiritualistic séance he had sometimes seen the face of a medium change, when some control took possession. His own nervousness and anxiety were becoming intolerable, and though the curiously surly attitude of his friend certainly did not invite further interference, he felt that he actually must try to relieve the tension by one more remonstrance. But just as he had made up his mind to speak,

Charles suddenly sat down, not upon the settee which he had formerly chosen, but upon the Baron's chair in front of the table, and there he sat sluggish and irresponsive as ever, shading his eyes from the light.

"Get up, man, get up!" cried Henri. "Don't you know that that is the very chair in which it is said that the Baron sits? And", looking at his watch, "it is within a few moments of his time too!"

But Charles took no notice, and remained immovable. Uncontrollably excited, Henri rushed up to him and shook him by the shoulder, calling loudly to him:

"Wake up, wake up! what is the matter with you?"

Even as he was speaking the great clock in the turret outside began to strike the hour of midnight. A sudden sound—a sort of subdued crash for which he could not account—drew his attention towards one end of the room, and as his eye fell upon the great mirror, he saw reflected in it the little group of Charles and himself, strongly illuminated by the light of the great lamp on the table close to them. He saw his own startled visage, and Charles with his face shaded by his hand; but even as he watched the mirror, the other figure raised its head, and with a shock of horror he realized that the countenance reflected was not his friend's at all! It was the face of the Baron, just as they had seen it in his portrait, and he was in the very act of drawing the razor across his throat once more.

With a shout of terror Henri tore away his eyes from the mirror and looked down on the figure under his hand, to see unmistakably not his friend's face but the Baron's looking up at him with a diabolical grin of triumphant malice, even as he felt a torrent of blood flow down upon his hand. It seemed to Henri as though something gave way inside his brain, and he fell to the ground unconscious.

He was aroused at length by a hand upon his shoulder—a tremulous hand—and by an anxious voice asking him.

" Where is your friend? "

For a few moments he felt too confused to be capable of answering; but after a while collected his scattered wits and realized his position. He found himself lying on the floor of the Baron's room, close to the central table, and the old caretaker bending over him with a face full of agitation and anguish.

" Where is your friend, monsieur? " he asked again, " where is the other gentleman? "

The horrible events of the previous night came back to his mind with a rush, and he sat up and looked about him. Truly Charles was not to be seen, nor was there any trace of the ghastly figure which had repeated the Baron's suicide. He could give no answer to the old man's question, but after a time he became collected enough to tell his story. The old care-taker was full of lamentations, and wrung his hands as though distracted, declaring over and over again that he had known from the first that evil would come from this mad adventure, and blaming himself most severely for having ever allowed himself to become a party to it, even in the most indirect manner.

"It is strange and terrible that your friend should thus have disappeared", he cried.

"Yes", said Henri; "we must search the house for him. He may have been smitten by terror; he may have fled and concealed himself; he may have fainted just as I did, but in some other room. Let us go and search."

"But you yourself, monsieur—you are wounded, are you not?" queried the old man.

"No," replied Henri, "I think not; I feel nothing but great weakness and trembling."

"But", said the old man, "look at your hand; it is covered with blood!"

To his great horror Henri saw that this was so. The blood of the Baron or of Charles (for he knew not what was the truth of it) had flowed over his hand as the suicide was repeated, and that blood remained—a ghastly witness of the reality of that awful scene!

"Bring me water," he cried to the old man, "bring me water at once, or I shall cut my hand off."

The old man quickly fetched him a bowl of water from a well close by, and he soon removed those ill-omened stains; yet though they yielded to the water in the ordinary way, though to the sight they had disappeared, he felt as though they were still there, as though his hand could never be clean again. Slowly, because he was very weak, they passed from room to room of the old house, seeking for any trace of Charles, but in vain. They saw their own foot-marks in the dust, the foot-marks which they had made when they went over the house the day before; but they saw no others, and found no trace of any sort of the missing man.

"He must have been carried away by the devil!" cried the old care-taker.

They searched the nearest part of the gardens also; but Henri's strength failed him, and this work was left uncompleted, for he resolved first to return to the town and to make certain enquiries. But before leaving him, he turned to the old man and said to him impressively:

"Do not grieve; you have done nothing but what is right. All through, you did your very 'best to persuade us not to undertake this mad experiment, but we would not be warned. You are in no way responsible if any harm has come from it. I do not know where my friend is; I do not understand at all the events of last night; but I decline altogether to believe that my friend has been carried off by the devil, as you think. If he saw what I saw—but how could he have seen it when it was he himself? I do not understand; but he may have been frightened, he may have rushed away. I may yet find him; I hope so; but in any case be assured of this. You at least have nothing with which to reproach yourself, and I shall never reproach you; nor shall I ever say anything of the occurrence of last night unless I am compelled to do so in my friend's interest. I shall go into the village now; before I leave it I will see you again if I have any news to give."

And so, shaking hands with the old man, he left him somewhat comforted.

As he walked slowly townwards his mind was filled with agitated reflections. He felt scarcely yet capable of connected thought or of reasoning, and indeed this thing was a nightmare which seemed to defy reason. He could not even think what he ought to do, or whether he should give notice to the authorities of the disappearance of his friend.

Before he had come to any decision he found himself approaching the hotel, and he made his way to his room without attracting attention. He went to Charles's room but there was no sign of him, nor had his bed been slept in. Henri returned to his own room and threw himself upon a couch, for it seemed to him that most of all he needed rest—that he must sleep before he would be capable of facing this strange and terrible emergency. He felt that something should be done, and done at once, and yet he could do nothing, nor did he even know what should be done. He knew he needed sleep, and yet his anxiety would not let him sleep. And so he lay for awhile, wondering vaguely what would come of it all.

His wearied body was almost yielding to slumber, when suddenly the door was thrown open and there before him stood Charles in his ordinary dress, looking precisely as though nothing had happened!

Henri sprang to his feet, crying something wildly and incoherently, rushed up to the astonished Charles and grasped his arm to see if indeed it was he or only an hallucination of his half-maddened brain.

" My dear fellow, what in the world is the matter with you?" said Charles. " What has happened?"

" Thank God, it is you ", said Henri, " and that you look quite well again; but surely I should rather ask *you* what happened and where you went last night, when you so mysteriously disappeared."

"Disappeared!" said Charles. "What do you mean? I left you at about six o'clock, you know and you were to call at my friend's house at half-past ten, but you never came, and I was really anxious about you."

"Never came!" said Henri. "What do *you* mean? Certainly I came; I met you—"

"What!" interrupted Charles, "You met me? But I have never seen you since I left this hotel at six o'clock. There is some mystery here, and you look as though it had been a terrible one. Sit down now, and tell me all about it."

"I will," said Henri; "but first tell me where you have spent the night."

"At my friend's house, of course", said Charles. "I dined with my friend as I intended, but unfortunately after dinner a slight faintness came over me. Nothing serious—no; but it lasted some time, and left me feeling weak and tottering, and my friends insisted that I should not think under such circumstances of attempting our adventure, nor even of trying to make my way back to the hotel until after a night's rest. They seized upon me with kindly fussiness, they put me to bed in their spare room, and administered cordials to me, assuring me that when you called they would explain everything to you and, if I were still awake, would bring you up to my bedside. But long before you were due, I had fallen asleep under the influence of their medicine. I slept until this morning, and awoke feeling perfectly refreshed and strong and well again. Having heard that you had not come after all, I was anxious to see what was the matter, so I came to the hotel as soon as possible, and here I am! I am all impatience to hear your story."

Henri told it as well as he could, to the accompaniment of many exclamations of wonder from Charles, and then they began gradually to try to construct some sort of a theory as to what had really happened. One thing at least seemed clear; that terrible Baron had somehow or other foreseen their intention, perhaps had invisibly accompanied them during their examination of his house in the afternoon, and then had resolved to lure Henri to what might very well have been his destruction, by taking the place of his friend, upon whose company and assistance he was depending for the due carrying out of his plan. Perhaps, indeed, the Baron may somehow or other have caused Charles's indisposition; at any rate he unquestionably decided to take advantage of it by personating him; and it is equally certain that he kept up his materialization for so long a time by draining away Henri's strength.

In this very fact lay the peculiar horror of the situation—that Henri himself had felt unusually nervous, and certainly would not have undertaken the investigation but for the presence and support of his friend; and yet at the critical moment, when above all things support was needed, that friend himself proved to be the apparition! They talked over the matter for hours, but they could make nothing more of it than this. On one point at least they both heartily agreed, that they desired to make no further investigations into the mystery of the Baron's room.

Nevertheless, they felt that they owed it to their good old friend, the care-taker, to pay one more visit to his cottage, and to relieve his mind as to the consequences of their strange adventure. But they took care to make that visit at high noon, and nothing would have induced either of them to enter that fatal house again. The old care-taker had been sunk in the blackest despair; but when he saw them both safe and well, he blessed God fervently and declared that a great weight was lifted from his heart, for he had been feeling all morning that he should never forgive himself for his share in the events of the previous night.

They told him their story, for they felt that that at least was due to him. They asked particularly whether he had seen Monsieur Charles the night before, and whether he had detected any difference in him, but the old man said:

" No, I did not notice the second gentleman particularly; now I come to think of it, it is true that Monsieur Charles stood back away from the light that shone out through the door, but I took no particular notice of this, since I was myself in a very agitated frame of mind." And then he broke forth again in rhapsodies of relief that after all there was no blood upon his soul, since they were both safe and well.

They pressed on him a still further gift, assuring him when he protested that the experience through which they had passed was indeed well worth it to them; but though he was much the richer for this strange adventure, he asserted most fervently that never again under any circumstances whatever, not even for all the wealth of the Rothschilds, should any one with his consent spend a night in the Baron's room.

SAVED BY A GHOST

CHAPTER I

EXPLANATORY

I, VICTOR KING-NORMAN, am an old man now, and the events of my boyhood, of which I am about to write, lie half a century behind me. But even now it is painful to recall them, and I should not have disinterred them from the grave of time and renewed their vivid sensations, but for a request from an honoured friend whose wish is law to me. In obedience to that command I tell my tale, suppressing only the true names of some of the actors in the drama.

My father, Norman King-Norman, had been a man of considerable reputation in London in his youth, in the days of King William IV of somewhat inglorious memory. After he married my mother he disappeared altogether from the London firmament of which he had been a luminary, and lived all the year round at Norman Hall, his ancestral home in the north country.

When railways began to be heard of, he was keenly interested in them, foresaw a magnificent future for them, and invested much of his fortune in them. When I was thirteen years of age he had become the leading director of a certain railway then in course of construction in South America, and in connection with it he found it necessary to visit that continent—a much more serious voyage in those days of paddle-wheel steamers than it is now.

He took with him his family, consisting of my mother, myself, and my younger brother Gerald— a child of about seven years. We took a house at the seaport town which was the terminus of the railway, and resided there during the greater part of our stay in the country; but my father's business frequently took him into the interior, to the unfinished part of the line. I believe that the contractors found themselves unable for some reason to carry on the work, and that consequently my father, on behalf of the Company, practically took the completion of the line out of their hands; at any rate, whether I am correct as to the business details or not, I know that after the first few months his absences from the town were frequent and prolonged.

On several of these expeditions I was, to my great delight, permitted to accompany him; and once, on the memorable occasion whose history I am about to relate, my little brother Gerald was also allowed to join the party. The mother's anxious eye had detected—or she fancied so—some slight sign of diminished strength in the little boy; and it was thought that the entire change of life involved in a few days camping-out " up country " would be beneficial to him.

Before I can make my story intelligible to those who have not lived in South America, it will be necessary for me briefly to explain the social conditions of that marvellous continent. There are—or were at the time of which I speak—four principal races among the inhabitants of that part of the country in which lies the scene of my tale.

First came the descendants of the Spanish and Portuguese conquerors—a haughty, indolent race; a race courtly and hospitable, by no means without its good qualities, but yet one whose strongest characteristic was an immeasurable contempt (or the affectation of it) for all other races whatsoever.

Next came the Red Indians—the earlier lords of the soil; of these many tribes had adopted a kind of squalid semi-civilization, but many others were still savages untamed and untamable—men who regarded work of any kind as the deepest degradation—who hated the white man with a traditional, unrelenting hatred, and (strange though it may seem) more than reciprocated the boundless contempt of the blue-blooded hidalgo of Spain. It will no doubt be incomprehensible to many of us that a half-naked savage can entertain any other feeling than envy for our superior civilization, however much he may dislike us; but I can only say that the quite genuine and unaffected feeling of the Red Indian towards the white man is pure and unmitigated contempt. It is not flattering to our self-love, but it is absolutely true for all that; and an uncomfortable suspicion *will* sometimes creep in that there are aspects of the case in which his feeling is—well, not so very unreasonable.

Third came the Negro race—no inconsiderable portion of the populations, and chiefly in a state of slavery, though the Government was doing all in its power to remove that curse from its territories; and last and worst came what were called the half-breeds or half-castes—a mixed race which seemed, as mixed races sometimes do, to combine all the worst qualities of both its parent stocks. Indian, Spaniard, and Negro alike despised them; and they in turn regarded all alike with a virulent hatred. So strong were these feelings that, when it came to enlistment in the army, the other races absolutely declined to serve in the same regiment with the half-castes, and these people therefore had to be drafted into regiments by themselves, so that there existed in the army regiments of both types, and their feelings towards each other were decidedly unfriendly.

At the time when my story begins these feelings of scarcely-veiled hostility had at last broken out into actual warfare. I forget what was made the excuse for the outbreak; some orders which were given to the half-caste regiments offended their dignity in some way, and there was an open mutiny. Four of these regiments marched off under the leadership of a man named Martinez, an officer, not without a certain amount of ability, but bearing an atrociously bad reputation. He was popularly credited with having broken over and over again every commandment in the decalogue; but whether all this was true or fabulous, it was at least certain that he was a man of vicious temper and abominable cruelty. Nevertheless he was said to be a good though unscrupulous leader, and there was a certain dash about him which made men of his own race follow him.

The affair ought to have been nothing but a petty mutiny quickly suppressed, and indeed that was what the Government wished us to believe with regard to it. The Government of any South American State is usually in a rather precarious condition, and most of its subjects are generally ready on very slight provocation to make an

12

attempt to overturn it; so the disaffection spread and became quite a rebellion. In the part of the country where we were, little was known of the movements of the insurgents; and, as I have said, it was the policy of the Government to minimize the whole affair and assure us that it was quite unimportant.

Later, when everything was over, it transpired that Martinez had concocted a plot of considerable ingenuity, and had contrived by all kinds of specious promises to induce several of the savage Indian tribes to join him. The two parties to this precious conspiracy were each playing false with the other; the ideas of the half-breeds were to utilize the Indians to help them to massacre the whites, and then to turn upon their partners and murder them in turn, and thus consolidate their power. The idea of the Red Indians on the other hand was that they could utilize the mutinous regiments to help them to drive the white men into the sea, after which it would be quite easy to massacre the half-breeds, and so regain the country for themselves.

It never occurred to us that any danger from the insurgents could menace our little expedition into the interior. Whatever fighting there was, was going on some hundreds of miles to the south, and the whole of our part of the country was perfectly free from it. But nevertheless we were destined to see much more of the struggle than we wanted, as my story will presently show.

The railway line ran through great tracts of primeval forest; and a South American forest is like no other in the world. Trees two hundred feet high and wide-spreading in proportion, literally one mass of blazing colour; domes of blue or scarlet or orange, and great creepers, thick as a man's leg, hanging from tree to tree, extending often for hundreds of feet, and covered with flowers even more splendid than those of the trees themselves. It was a favourite game with the children to choose each one of these giant creepers, and try in spite of its entanglements to trace it out to its end—the boy who had chosen the longest creeper being of course the winner. It was a veritable fairyland, unequalled in its marvellous beauty, but much too thickly inhabited for human comfort.

Precisely because men are so few, the non-human inhabitants flourish to a degree unknown elsewhere, and a large proportion of them are dangerous to man. Splendid creatures, many of them, but distinctly uncomfortable neighbours. The jaguar, more beautiful and kingly-looking even than the royal tiger of India, but equally dangerous; the boa-constrictor, the largest snake in the world, often thirty feet long and as thick as a man's thigh; the alligator, deadly as the shark of the ocean, swarming in every river and pool; all these and many other creatures make the conditions of human life somewhat arduous in those marvellous South American forests.

Full of birds, too, are they, alive with colours equalling those of the flowers; parrots of all kinds; huge screaming macaws, painted crudely and gorgeously in scarlet and blue and yellow; tiny humming-birds, no larger than the bumble-bee, but glowing with ruby and emerald like actual living jewels; hundreds of varieties all resplendent in hue, but songless, except for the deep ringing bell-like note of the *campanero*; all kinds of strange-looking creatures, wondrous in colour but always with something bizzare about them, something unlike what is seen in any other land.

But it is the insect world above all others which forces itself upon the attention of a visitor, and usually unpleasantly. The tarantula and the scorpion are its aristocracy—not properly insects at all; huge ants, in countless millions, which start out upon mysterious migrations and turn aside for nothing; chigoes, uncomfortable little creatures which get under one's toe-nails and lay tiny little bags full of eggs, which have to be cut out by the servants each evening before one goes to bed. Assuredly the insect world is ever with us, and we usually wish that it was not.

Nevertheless, there was little of danger about our invasion of these primeval forests, for we were undertaking it under unusually favourable conditions. The small army of labourers who were working at the end of the line gave us the advantage of company. None of the larger wild beasts would come into the neighbourhood of so great a crowd of men, and we learnt by dire experience how to deal with the smaller beasts. Along with us as a kind of valet and general guardian came our faithful Negro servant Tito. He had been presented to us as a slave, but we had freed him, and consequently he was over-flowing with gratitude.

The railway was a mere trench cut through the forest, almost in a straight line, for at this stage no intermediate station had as yet been erected, and though it passed in the neighbourhood of several villages, none of them were actually in sight from it, so there was nothing to prevent a clear run. I remember on one occasion, a few weeks before that of which I am writing, I had myself a very exciting experience on that same line.

One day, when we were away at the end of the line just seventy-five miles from the terminus, news reached us through the arrival of a brother of one of the labourers that very serious defalcations had taken place in the office at the terminus, and that the defaulting cashier was departing with his plunder by a certain steamer bound for Europe, which was due to start on that very day. The news arrived just an hour before the time for the sailing of the mail-steamer, and my father was in despair as to what to do. There were no telegraphs in those days, and a runner would take thirty hours to cover the distance, even going along the newly-made railway line.

We had an engine with us, but it was what is called a contractor's engine, not built for any high speeds; and even so, its regular driver was down that day with fever, and the young lad who was in charge of it, though he managed well enough to pull a few trucks up and down, was quite incapable of trying a record run with it. My father did not know how to manage the locomotive, and besides, it would have been a very serious matter for him to leave just then; but fortunately I, with a boy's fancy for machinery, had learnt to understand the engine pretty well, and had driven it many times, though only for short distances.

I at once offered to try to make the run in time to stop the steamer, and somehow felt certain that I could do it, although my father thought it quite impossible. Moments were flying, however, and there was little time to discuss the matter, so he consented to my making the attempt, though he thought it foredoomed to failure. The engine had steam up, and a few moments sufficed to load it with coal, and make sure that its tanks were full; and then off I started, with the boy who had previously driven the engine as a fireman. The run was a most exciting one; I pushed that engine to its utmost speed, and it was fortunate for me that on the whole the line was fairly straight, for I was in no mood to slacken much for curves. Suffice it to say that I did the distance in the time, though I arrived with the plates of the engine red-hot.

As soon as we reached the terminus, I jumped off and rushed up to the signal-tower on the hill, the official in charge of which was well known to me; and thankful I was to see the mail-steamer still lying in the bay, though she was even already getting up her anchors. Under my instructions, my friend the official at once ran up a signal imperatively calling upon the steamer to wait. Meantime I ran down the hill to the port authorities, and very soon a boat with quite an imposing array of police and other officials was being rowed out rapidly towards the steamer.

These port officials knew my father well as the consignee of large cargoes of rails and other materials, and so when once I reached the place my task was an easy one. Even the captain of the steamer knew me, and when he understood the gravity of the emergency he forgave me for delaying him.

The defaulting cashier was at once arrested in spite of his excited protests, and haled ashore to prison, all the money being duly recovered. I believe I considerably damaged that engine by reckless over-driving; but the amount at stake was large enough to condone that trifling irregularity.

It was my father's custom to have a small wooden cabin built for him out at the end of the line, and live in it for a few days until the line had been constructed to a point which he found inconveniently far from it. Then he would have another similar cabin erected a little further along. Wood was so abundant that it was not worth while to carry the logs from one such halting place to another, even though it was only a few miles further on. There were generally plenty of logs lying on the ground, so some trees could be quickly chopped down and a new cabin put up at the cost of very little labour.

The usual plan was to choose logs perhaps a foot in diameter and split them in half longitudinally and in this way a rough hut was made quite strong enough to keep out any wild beasts known in that country, though there were of course many cracks between the logs, through which came plenty of light and air. Generally such as cabin was made without a window, but with a rough door—a door which had no hinges, but was kept in its place during the night by a heavy wooden bar which prevented it from falling inwards. In the daytime the door was laid aside and the empty place served as a window. My father had a rough table for his office work, and we sat about on stumps or lay on the floor, as fancy dictated.

CHAPTER II

ATTACKED BY THE INDIANS

On the day on which my story begins, this hut happened to be erected at one end of a sort of glade or open place in the forest. Behind and on each side of the hut, the forest was not more than twenty yards away, but in front of its door the glade sloped gently down to the banks of a little stream perhaps a hundred and fifty yards away. Away beyond that stream, but concealed from view from the hut by great clumps of trees and a rise in the ground, was the end (for the time being) of the railway, where a crowd of men were busily working.

The men usually took a short siesta in the middle of the day, according to the custom of the country, and we sometimes tried to do so too; but, not being used to it, I at least could never get to sleep. This siesta was still in progress, though if I recollect rightly, it was about the time of its conclusion. My father sat writing at his table; I lay on the floor reading a story, and little Gerald was playing some childish game away in a corner. The servant Tito was absent on some of his work; at any rate he was not in the cabin or visible from it.

Suddenly the quiet of tropical noon was broken by a volley of rifle-shots—a most astounding phenomenon, for so far as we knew there was not a rifle except our own within fifty miles at least. We sprang to our feet, and my father went to the door and looked out down the glade. As I have said, the spot where the men were working was not actually visible from our door; so, as there was nothing unusual to be seen, my father took his rifle from the corner where it leaned, and started to see what was the matter. I snatched up my rifle also—for I also had one; in that wild country even little Gerald never went out without his tiny revolver stuck in his belt, and I habitually carried a brace of Colts, and took a rifle with me whenever I went out for a walk. And these precautions were by no means unnecessary, for, to say nothing of human inhabitants, dangerous wild animals came down quite close to the houses even on the outskirts of the town. Why, one morning I saw—but that is another story, as Rudyard Kipling so often says.

We were hardly outside the door when one of our labourers appeared from behind the clump of trees near the stream, running wildly. When he saw us he uttered a shout, but we could not understand what he said, and before he had time to speak again another rifle-shot rang out, and he threw up his arms and fell dead. Immediately there burst into view at the bottom of the glade a great crowd of painted savages, who waved their weapons and emitted blood-curdling yells. Several shots were fired at us, but fortunately we were untouched, and we at once retired into the hut and put the door into its place, slipping in the heavy bar behind it. Then quite calmly my father remarked to me, as I stood there with my rifle still in my hand:

" You take the crack to the left of the door, and I will take this on the right. Rifles first; then pistols. We must kill as many as we can before they reach the hut. Steady, now; we cannot afford to miss."

We had not then the quick-firing guns of the present day; but still ten of those Red Indians fell before they had come more than half-way up the rise. Some word of command was shouted, and in an instant they dashed into cover at each side of the glade, and for the moment disappeared from our sight. Still watching through the crack, my father said:

" This gives us a moment's respite. Load again; have everything ready, and all your ammunition where you can reach it in a moment. They will be on us again directly."

" But, father," said I, " who are they, and what is it all about, and why do they come here attacking us in this mad way? We have done them no harm."

"I don't know, my boy," he said; "and, as far as I can see, it does not seem very likely that we ever shall know, because whatever they want, and however they come here, we cannot hope to hold this place against a crowd like that; and all that we can do is to sell our lives as dearly as possible. We are a hundred miles from the nearest help, and long before it can get here they will have disposed of us. I should not care for that, but that we have little Gerald with us. Why in the world did I bring him just this time and no other? and then *this* must happen!"

"What do you suppose has become of the men—the labourers?" said I.

"They must have been all killed," replied my father, "in that volley that we heard. That is clear, because if any were left they would certainly have run in this direction, to try to take refuge with us."

"But I do not see why they should kill them, or why they come after us," I objected.

"No," said my father, "I do not understand it either; but at least this is certain, that they are in their war-paint, and that always means they have started out with the intention to kill, and that they will fight to the death. No one can tell the reasons on which these barbarians act."

At this moment we were interrupted by another loud yell, and the whole band of savages, who had come closer to us under cover of the forest, rushed out upon us simultaneously from both sides. Man after man fell, but they dashed up to the hut bravely enough, and threw themselves against the door. Fortunately the bar held, and, as they soon saw that they could do nothing to us, and were absolutely exposed to our fire, with another great shout they dashed back again into shelter.

So far we had escaped unhurt, while quite a number of corpses lay round the hut, for even little Gerald had taken his part bravely, and had shot at least two of the savages, besides wounding another. On my side one fierce-looking fellow had thrust the muzzle of his rifle through one of the cracks. I leaped to one side, seized it just as he discharged it, and fired my revolver over it straight in the face of its owner, who fell back with a groan, leaving the rifle projecting through the crack.

His shot filled the hut with smoke, but otherwise did us no harm. When they had fled into the woods I wanted to unbolt the door in order to take in that rifle, but my father would not allow it, saying that the Indians were certainly watching us from the woods, and that it would be an unnecessary exposure. Also he pointed out that the rifle would be of no use to us, even after we got it, as we were already armed and our ammunition would not fit it. It was a queer old muzzle-loader, fired with a percussion cap, and would certainly, as my father said, have been of no use to us; yet I relinquished that trophy with great reluctance, even though I knew quite well that the probabilities were that we should never live to exhibit it to anybody. So we pushed the rifle out, and let it fall among the bodies outside.

We had repulsed the attack, certainly, and so far we were unhurt, while the enemy had suffered considerable loss. We had gained but a barren victory, however, and we were under no illusions as to the gravity of our situation. We had with us a fair supply of ammunition, and, entrenched as we were, behind—not boards, but—heavy logs which were bullet-proof, we might possibly hold our own against another such attack or even several such, though a chance bullet might at any moment find its way through a crack and lay one of us low. But we had no food whatever (save, I think, half a box of biscuits); and, worse still, we had only a half-emptied bottle of water. Our meals were under ordinary circumstances cooked for us by the missing Tito, but his primitive culinary arrangements were usually made out in the open or under a tree, and such stores of food as we had with us were kept with other stores down in the sheds near the railway line, so that if the savages chose simply to sit down and besiege us, there could be only one end to the affair.

Our conversation, as may be imagined, was not very hopeful. One thing alone seemed to occupy my father's mind—regret that he had brought my younger brother into this terrible position, and sorrow for the shock that the little boy's inevitable death must produce upon his loving mother. We speculated ceaselessly as to why these Indians were attacking us, and (more practically) as to what they were likely to do next, though the answers to these questions could hardly have been of any great importance to us. Whatever were their reasons, that they were going to kill us seemed certain. There appeared to be not the slightest loophole of escape, and absolutely the only thing that we could do on our side was to make the inevitable result as difficult for them as possible, and to exact from them as heavy a price for their victory as lay in our power.

Now ensued a long period of waiting, which was far more trying to our nerves (to mine at least) than the exciting time of the attack. All was silent in the forest around us, but unfortunately we knew well that that silence did not indicate that the Indians had abandoned us. After a long time, indeed, we heard a sound of chopping, and marvelled much what our enemies might be doing. Presently we discovered the meaning of the sound, for quite suddenly—in a flash, as it were—the silence changed into a pandemonium of sound, the savages rushing yelling upon the hut once more, madly and uselessly discharging their rifles at it as they ran forward. As before, we fired as rapidly as we could, and had already accounted for several of the attacking party, when my father shouted across to me:

" Here, this way. Aim only at those men with the log."

Then I saw that six or eight of the Indians were carrying between them a huge log, which they evidently intended to use as a battering-ram to break in our door, which no doubt with so great a weight they could easily have done. But, though they had only some twenty yards to bring the thing, it did not reach us; my father's quick grasp of their intention foiled their plan for this time, at any rate, for we concentrated the fire of our revolvers upon those who were bearing the tree-trunk, and when they had gone half the distance already half of them were down, and the remainder found the weight too great for them. Others sprang forward bravely to take their places, but they were too late to catch the falling log, and when once it lay on the ground it was death for any man to approach it. Once more our assailants broke and fled in confusion. Once more we were left to exult over a temporary victory,

13

and quite a pile of bodies lay upon and around their battering-ram.

This time, however, we had had the narrowest of escapes, for while my father and I were concentrating our attention upon those who surrounded the battering-ram, another plumed warrior had crept to the back of the hut, thrust the muzzle of his gun through a crack, and fired it at us from behind. He missed us, though but by a hair's breadth, and we found the bullet afterwards, embedded in one of the logs by the door. Our little Gerald had seen him and fired at him; indeed it is probable that it was his shrill shout of warning which deflected the Indian's aim. Gerald reported that he had not killed the man, but only wounded him, for though he staggered back and seemed badly hurt, he was yet able to crawl off into the forest. Our foes had lost heavily in their three attempts to capture us, but we knew that that would make them all the more determined that we should on no account escape.

Now there began for us a period of the most trying suspense. Hour after hour passed by, and nothing whatever occurred. We could not hope that they had given up their prey; we knew well enough that their chiefs had been dismayed by the slaughter of their men, and that they had decided to wait until darkness gave them a better opportunity. For myself, I know that I wished that they would attack us again, that they would continue attacking us, for anything seemed to me to be better than that dreadful waiting for certain death. Of course we speculated as to where poor Tito was, and how they had killed him; as to how the attack upon the workmen had been arranged; and what had happened to the foreman, a big powerful Scotchman, who must surely have been taken unawares, or he would have contrived to give a good account of almost any number of the savages. We thought of the mother at home and wondered whether any news of our fate would ever reach her, considering that there seemed to be no one left to tell the tale.

We were, I believe, what would be called religious people, yet I do not recollect that at this crisis of our fate we talked much about religious subjects. Once only, so far as I remember, did my father refer to such matters.

"Well, boys," he said, "you are young to have to die like this, before you have seen anything of life, and I am sorry that I brought you with me. But it is no use being sorry; and who could have foreseen this? But remember we are in God's hands, and nothing can happen to us without His knowledge and whatever is His will for us, somehow or other that is the best for us, and if we die bravely, as Englishmen should, you may be sure that somehow we are serving Him in doing it, and when we meet Him hereafter it will matter very little when or how we died, will it? "

And I think that, young as we were, we were inspired by his example, and we were chiefly comforted by the thought that at least we were dying together.

Time wore on, and at last the quick darkness of the tropics fell upon us. I think the strain of waiting had told upon us all. I know that I had several times caught myself nodding, and I think that little Gerald was, for a time at least, sound asleep; but my father never relaxed his watch for a moment. When the darkness had fallen, and the sounds of tropical night were all around us, he gave us a few words of kindly encouragement, and for the first time made a suggestion which seemed to be inspired by the faintest gleam of hope.

"Boys," he said, "I do not know what they are doing, but if they do not show themselves soon I shall open the door as silently as possible, and we will try to slip off among the trees."

"But," I objected, "surely, father, they will be watching us on all sides."

"Yes," said my father, "most likely they are, but at least there is just a chance that we might get through. At the worst, if we fail, they can only kill us, and that is certainly what will happen to to us if we stay here."

When he said this I was all on fire to try the experiment at once; but then came to me the awful thought that perhaps we might not all escape, but that one of us might be killed; and suppose that one should be my father, what then should Gerald and I do? Or suppose it should be little Gerald, what use would my life be to me? I said nothing of these thoughts, but my enthusiasm for the plan was damped.

However, our ferocious enemies gave us no opportunity of putting it into execution. Suddenly out of the darkness came something like a stream of fire, and then in rapid succession another and another, and it seemed as though they fell upon the roof of our hut. For a moment we could not imagine what they were, but very soon the ingenuity of the savages dawned upon us. Though the walls of our hut were made of heavy half-logs deeply set in the ground, it was thatched only with palm-leaves. Our enemies had observed that vulnerable point, and were shooting on to the roof flaming arrows wrapped round with cotton steeped in oil.

In a few moments our roof was in a blaze, the hut was filled with blinding smoke, and the flaming fragments were falling all about us. We had to spring upon these fragments and stamp them out, or we should have been roasted to death; and while we were thus fighting for our lives with the flames, the Indians ran to where their battering-ram had fallen, picked it up and charged with it. With a tremendous crash the door and its bar broke from their supports, and in a moment we were surrounded by our foes. We could hardly see through the smoke, but already most of the burning thatch had fallen, and the onrush of the savages trampled out the flames.

"Back to back," my father shouted, and in a moment somehow he and I and little Gerald were together in the centre of the hut, in the midst of an evil-smelling mass of red men, who seemed to be charging upon us simultaneously from all sides. Even then our pistols rang out, and I know that one or two at least went down upon my side; but I received a heavy blow upon the head from behind, and then I knew no more for a while of what was happening.

After a time (how long a time I have no means of knowing) I came to myself again; but, as it seems to me in trying to remember it, only very slowly and confusedly. At first I was conscious of a vague sense of pain, of a curious persistent jolting and a strong desire that the jolting would stop, and let me be at peace. It continued, however, and the sense of discomfort increased, and presently I became dimly conscious that I was moving in some way, or rather being carried in some peculiarly awkward and uncomfortable fashion. I think I had no memory for quite a long time of the fight or the Indians, or indeed of anything; and I may have remained in this condition of semi-stupor for a long period. It seemed like interminable ages to me, yet of course it may really have been but a few minutes (I have no means of knowing); but as my senses gradually reasserted themselves, I felt that at intervals I was being roughly pushed and scratched and struck by something from above, while I was confined in some uncomfortable way from beneath.

I am trying to describe the sensations of my recovery as well as I can, and yet I cannot really express them, for it was all indescribably vague and cloudy, and I seemed quite incapable of assigning causes to these sensations, or of understanding what was happening to me. But somehow by degrees it dawned upon me that I was upon the back of a horse or a mule, that the horrible jolting was caused by his stumbling over what seemed to be very uneven ground, and that the blows and scratches came to me from the low hanging branches of the trees under which we were passing.

I think it was when I had got about as far as this, that my consciousness seemed to return to me with a kind of jerk, to wake up again within me suddenly, and I realized that I was bound upon the back of this animal, that he was one of a large number of similar creatures, some of which were loaded with what seemed to be bales of goods, while others were ridden by the Indians. I saw also that many Indians were all about us on foot. And then with a shock, memory fully returned to me, and I realized that I must have been stunned by a blow in the burning hut, and that instead of killing me on the spot these Indians were carrying me off as a prisoner.

We were pushing through the forest at a good speed, and there under the trees the darkness was impenetrable. But almost as soon as my senses had fully returned to me we came out into a sort of clearing, where I could dimly see the mob of mounted and running savages which surrounded me. My first thought was, " Is my father also a prisoner? " And I raised a shout of " Father "! At least I tried to make it a shout, though I dare say in reality it was but a feeble cry. A moment of terrible suspense, and then a great wave of thankfulness came over me as I heard his cheery voice exclaim in reply from somewhere amidst the dusky mass in front of me:

" Ha, my boy, you are alive then! " he cried; " are you much hurt? "

"No, I think not," I called in reply, "but my head feels queer. But are you hurt?"

I had only just time to hear "No" in reply, when an Indian thrust his face into mine and savagely told me to be silent, and at the same time I saw some sort of struggle taking place in front, which suggested that they were closing round my father and trying to keep him quiet also. The man who had checked me had spoken in a kind of bastard Spanish—half Spanish, half Portuguese, but spoken with a curious thick guttural accent that made it wellnigh incomprehensible; but when the ruffians round me spoke to one another, which was very rarely, they did so in some language of their own of which I knew nothing.

I could chatter well enough with the Negroes in the curious lingua franca which they speak, and I tried in that to ask the Indians around me where they were taking us, and where my little brother was; but they either did not or would not understand me. At any rate they made no reply further than roughly to repeat the command to be silent when I tried to shout to my father once more. For some time after this I was in anxiety concerning the fate of little Gerald, but at last as we were crossing an open space I had the great joy of seeing him alive and apparently unhurt. A man who seemed of some consequence among the Indians was holding him in front of him as he rode, seated on the neck of his horse. I called to him at once to ask if he was hurt, and he called back :

"No, not much," and, I think, asked after me. But the man who was holding him shook him roughly and ordered him to be quiet. Now that my mind was relieved as to the fate of my father and brother, I had leisure to consider my own condition, and it certainly did not improve on consideration. I found that I had been stripped absolutely naked, that my wrists were fastened together tightly behind me, and that my ankles were secured by a rope or thong which passed under the body of my steed.

In front of me was some sort of pack or roll of blankets, and to this also I was bound, apparently by the rope which tied it on to the horse. In my insensible condition I suppose I must have lain on this roll, tied to it as though I had myself been simply another package ; and even now that I had come to myself I was unable to sit up and ride properly, or to extend a hand to save myself from striking against the lower branches of the trees under which we passed. Altogether my position was a vilely uncomfortable one, and when I add to that the fact that my head ached abominably from the blow which had stunned me, it will readily be understood that I was not in especially good spirits.

As far as I was able to think connectedly, I believe that I spent most of my time in wondering about the situation in which we found ourselves. Who could these Indians be, and what could be their objects in attacking us so savagely as they had done, and yet after all in taking us prisoners instead of killing us off-hand? I knew well enough, from plenty of stories that I had heard, that it was not their custom to take prisoners; and though while there is life there is hope, and it was at least an unexpected boon that our lives had been spared so far. I must admit that the more I reflected upon our probable future the less I liked the prospect.

It seems incredible, in such a hideously uncomfortable position, but I believe that I must actually have slept, or at least dozed; for I remember nothing of the dawning, yet it was full daylight when my steed stopped with a jerk, which woke me to the consciousness that we were out of that interminable forest at last. To my intense surprise I saw before me, not the wigwams of the Indians, but what appeared to be the tents of an army; and with that sight there came upon me a sudden gleam of hope, which oddly enough turned me absolutely sick. If here were military tents, surely here also must be civilized men, and since these Indians, instead of killing us, had brought us to this place, was there not possible some hope of escape after all? What it all meant I had no more idea than I had had before, but at least this was something quite different from the gruesome end to our ride which my fears had been prompting me to expect when I fell asleep.

CHAPTER III

AT THE CAMP OF MARTINEZ

THE Indians now began to unload the horses and to turn them out to graze, and among others they untied the rope that bound me to the bundle in front of me, and also that which fastened my ankles underneath the body of the horse. They did not, however, untie the cord which bound my wrists, and they simply dropped me on the ground among the other bales, and paid but little further attention to me. Perhaps it was just as well, for I hardly think that I could have stood upon my feet, and I was well content to sit upon the ground for a while and try to steady my swimming head and stretch my cramped muscles.

My father and Gerald had also been dismounted with a similar lack of ceremony, but a man stood on each side of my father as he sat on the ground, and though no actual endeavour to bind us was made beyond the fastening of the wrists, it was quite evident that we were carefully guarded, and that the Indians had no intention of neglecting us, or giving us any opportunity of slipping away from them.

Still, they did not prevent my father from walking over to where I lay and sitting down on the ground beside me, though his guards followed him closely. My father spoke authoritatively to such as appeared to be the chief men among the Indians, demanding in his best Spanish (which I must admit was barely intelligible) what they meant by seizing us in this way, by stripping us of our clothes, and generally treating us thus disgracefully. The Indians, however, took no notice—possibly because they really did not understand; though they must have known in a general way what he was saying, for presently they threw over us a couple of dirty ponchos. Now in that part of the world the poncho of an Indian was nothing but a blanket with a hole in the middle, through which the proud possessor put his head; so regarded as garments these things were distinctly inadequate, but at least they were enormously better than nothing, though we made many grimaces at their filthiness.

My father proclaimed his intention of going to the nearest of the tents, and trying to open up communication with some civilized being; but this the Indians would not permit, and they were evidently prepared to use force if necessary to detain us where we were. So we soon agreed that it was better for us to remain quiet and let circumstances develop themselves, since it seemed reasonably evident that the Indians did not mean to kill us or further to ill-treat us, and it was also clear that the camp was not yet awakened, for no one was moving about but a few sentinels.

The nearest tent to us was a large one, which was set quite apart from the others, higher up than they, and close to the edge of the forest. I remember it occurred to me that the scene in front of us had a certain resemblance to the little glade in which our hut had been erected, except that it was on a much larger scale. The forest lay behind us, and the larger tent which I have described stood with its back to it, something in the same way as our cabin had done. Down before it stretched a wide plain covered with the tents of the soldiers, and far away at the bottom I could see the gleaming waters of stream. It was not difficult to infer that this must be the tent of the general, or whatever the officer in charge of this body of troops was called, for a special sentinel marched up and down a short beat in front of it.

In a few minutes appeared a tall Indian with a magnificent plume of feathers, whom I at once recognized as having been among those who attacked us the night before. Indeed, as he came nearer, and I could look at him more closely, I realized that

I had seen him once before that also, though as he had then been dressed merely in the ordinary Indian fashion, I did not know him again at first in his war-paint and feathers. He had been pointed out to me in the streets of the town as a man of great power but exceedingly bad reputation, one who claimed the position of chief over all the Indians in that part of the country. He called himself by the name Anti-nahuel, which means, I am told, ' the tiger of the sun', and he claimed descent from the ancient Incas of Peru. My information had been to the effect that there was in reality no foundation whatever for this claim, and that it was not recognized by the Peruvian Indians. Indeed, when in Peru I had myself seen the man who was accepted as the legitimate descendant, and while I have no means of deciding between the rival claimants, I may at least say that that man looked gentle, dignified and kingly, while this man had a face which, though powerful, was full of revolting cruelty.

I was by no means reassured by my recognition of Antinahuel, for if half that I had heard of him was true, I could only wonder that after having fallen into his hands we were still alive. Still, we were alive, and the tents were evidence that we had some one else to deal with besides this relentless savage, so we waited with what patience we could. From the frequent glances directed by our guards and the others at the large tent, it seemed probable that we were waiting for some one to come out; perhaps for the general of this force to awaken.

Presently, by degrees, the camp arose from its slumbers, and we saw frowsy-looking soldiers coming out of the various tents and talking together. We noticed at once that there was an absence of the discipline which one would naturally have expected —that the men were not all roused at once by a reveille, but that they just seemed to wake as they chose. None of them, however, took any notice of us, or came up the hill to inspect us, from which we argued that they must be thoroughly accustomed to seeing the Indians in their war-paint —a sight which ordinarily would have instantly roused half-caste or Spanish natives into the wildest excitement.

Presently we could make out that some men dressed as officers were amongst the others, and a semblance of order began to show itself, some men trooping off down to the river with buckets. After a time, one who seemed to be a sort of leader among the Indians went down into the camp, and we saw him in conversation with one of the higher officers. After some few minutes' talk, they walked up the hill together and approached what we supposed to be the general's tent. Exchanging some password

14

with the sentry, who saluted him, the officer raised the flap of the tent and passed inside.

After an interval he came out again, accompanied by a choleric-looking little man who had evidently just been roused from sleep, and looked as though he resented it. He was dressed in a colonel's uniform, which, however, he wore in a slipshod, slovenly way. As he came out he was buckling his sword around his waist. As soon as he appeared, Antinahuel, who had, I suppose, been somewhere in the background all the time, came forward and exchanged with him a dignified salute.

We saw them speaking together, and it was evident from their glances in our direction that they were speaking of us. A crowd of soldiers was by this time gathering in that part of the camp nearest to us, apparently having realized that something unusual was going forward, but none of them ventured to approach very near to the tent, or to the group who were talking in front of it. The officer who had come up from the camp with the Indian turned towards them and shouted an order, and immediately four of his men came running up to him, received a few words of instruction, and then came quickly over to us, and motioned to us to rise and come with them. They did not touch us roughly in any way, but two of them ranged themselves one on each side of my father, another took charge of me and the fourth of little Gerald, and thus they marched us up before the little man, who was evidently the commander of this curiously undisciplined force.

We were certainly not very dignified in appearance; apart from our filthy ponchos we were absolutely naked, and not even decently clean; for the branches of the trees which had scratched and struck us as we rode hurriedly through them had covered us with smears and scratches, so that we presented a most disreputable appearance. Nevertheless, as soon as we were brought up before the commander, my father at once poured out upon him a most indignant complaint as to the way in which we had been treated, accused the Indians of the slaughter of his workmen, and threatened the dire vengeance of the British Government on the heads of all concerned.

His Spanish, as I have said, was distinctly faulty, and the effect of his outburst was much marred by the fact that at points where he became utterly explosive he generally had to turn to me for a word; for the fact was that, from running about perpetually among the Negro and Indian servants, I knew more of the *patois* of the country than he did. The little commander heard his tirade to the end, and then began to speak in reply with, I must admit, a praiseworthy courtesy. He began by expressing his deep regret at the 'accident' that had happened to us, assuring us that it was all a mistake.

" A mistake! " roared my father; " then it is a mistake for which somebody will have to pay heavily. Perhaps you do not realize that a number of men have been killed, seventy, eighty, a hundred men!"

The little commander shrugged his shoulders and spread out his hands, and assured us that no one could regret more than he the impetuosity of his Indian friends, but that in war these little mistakes would occasionally occur, and after all it was done, and it could not be undone.

My father was becoming more and more indignant, but he saw that this was not the time to discuss the question of eventual compensation or retribution, so he demanded that we should be instantly set free, and that our clothes should be returned to us, asserting that he was a British subject and did not propose to be treated in this way.

The little commander, with a patience really wonderful for him, considering what kind of man he was, replied that all this should be done, but that there was a little ceremony—a mere nothing —which it was necessary that we should go through first. He said that he had often heard of the English, and heard wonderful stories of their prodigious valour, and that while he regretted deeply, most deeply, that his Indian allies should have made the stupid error of mistaking us for Spaniards, and so putting us to all this deplorable inconvenience, yet on the other hand it was surely his good fortune which had brought us to him, in order that we might assist him in carrying out his plans.

He then gravely proceeded to offer to my father the command of one of the four regiments which he said he had with him, on consideration that we threw in our lot with him and took the oath of allegiance to him. He explained to us that he was General Martinez, and that the intolerable tyranny with which he and his race had been treated by the Spaniards had induced them to rise and throw off their yoke; that when this was done he himself intended to be the President or Dictator of the military republic which he should form, but he assured my father that in return for the help which he would now give him, he should receive a high post in this State of the future.

The cool assurance of all this amused us even under those circumstances, but it also aggravated my father still further, and he contrived to make the gist of his answer exceedingly clear, in spite of his broken Spanish. He declared that he, as a foreigner, had nothing whatever to do with the local disturbances of the country, and that he absolutely declined to take part in them either on one side or the other; nor would he under any circumstances take the oath of allegiance to one who was an insurgent against the lawfully established Government of his country.

It appeared to me that the little commander was getting decidedly annoyed, and his hand began to trifle ominously with his sword-hilt; but still he kept his temper wonderfully, and explained to my father that he had absolutely no choice in the matter. He was grieved to insist, he said, but the fact was that he had stolen a march upon his enemies, that he had shaken off their pursuit and had contrived, quite unknown to them, to move his regiments far to the north of where they were supposed to be, and that he intended to strike an unexpected blow at the town which was the terminus of our railway, descending upon it from the interior on the side where there were no fortifications, and taking its authorities entirely unawares. Now, through a concatenation of circumstances which no one could deplore more than he did, we had learned the secret of this plan of his, which must be known to no living person; and therefore (once more he shrugged his shoulders and spread out his hands) desolated though he was at the apparent interference with our liberty, he was absolutely compelled to put us instantly to death if we would not throw in our lot with him.

Still my father indignantly refused, asserting over and over again that as an Englishman he declined to take part in such affairs. The little commander's patience was rapidly giving out, and at last he spoke quite sharply and definitely:

"I can waste no more time, sir. You must choose at once; either you will swear fealty to me, according to our usual form, or you will die within the hour."

And he turned to his officer and ordered him to bring from his tent what was necessary for the taking of the oath. Two soldiers immediately brought out thence a little table, a large book, an inkstand and a pen, and at the same time the officer brought a large carved wooden crucifix— evidently stolen from some church—and threw it down on the ground in front of us.

In order to explain the presence of this last article I must mention one of the peculiarities of this formidable little man. Whatever he may have thought it wise to admit to his men, he knew perfectly well that the undertaking of driving the white people into the sea would be no light one, and that he could hope to achieve it only by retaining the most enthusiastic devotion of every one of the limited number of his followers. Furthermore he knew these followers well; he knew that they were steeped in superstition to the very marrow of their bones; and he knew well also the tremendous hold that the priests of the Catholic Church had in that semi-civilized country over the members of their flocks.

Perhaps the form of Christianity which was at that time prevalent in South America was the most degraded to be seen anywhere on earth; but that in no way interfered with the fact that the priests in reality ruled the country, and that in one way or another what they wanted was always done. He also knew well enough that the influence of the Church was hostile to him, not so much because he was a notorious evil-liver, as because the priests were very well satisfied with things as they were, and did not desire any interference with a Government which was thoroughly under their thumb.

In order to defeat this ecclesiastical influence he had hit upon a device which, though it had no other merits, might at least be described as bold and ingenious; with quaint blasphemy he had aped the celebrated declaration of King Nebuchadnezzar, and had made every one of his followers take a solemn oath that until the war was over and the country was in their hands they would speak to no priest, would enter no place of worship, and would offer no petition to God or man, except to himself. Each man had to swear this in front of Martinez himself, and in token of his temporary renunciation of his ancestral faith each was made to set his foot upon the crucifix. Every member of his motley crowd had gone through this ceremony, and now Martinez demanded that we should go through it also.

I need hardly say that we had not the remotest intention of doing anything of the kind. We were members of the Church of England, and not of that of Rome; but nevertheless my mother was a devoted follower of Dr. Pusey, with whom she was intimately acquainted, and I myself habitually wore a tiny ebony and silver crucifix around my neck underneath my clothes—the only thing, by the way, which the Red Indians had left me, because, I suppose, they recognized it as a magical symbol of the Christians, and may perhaps have feared its power. You may imagine therefore with what horror we regarded this impious suggestion of the general's; though I think there is no doubt that, even if there had been no crucifix in the case, we should equally have refused to be thus coerced into attaching ourselves to a cause with which we had no sympathy.

Martinez paid no attention to my father's indignant though ungrammatical protests, but curtly ordered him to put his foot upon the crucifix and to take the prescribed oath. I clearly remember the thought passing through my mind: "What in the world will my father do now?" for I never even dreamt of the possibility of his complying with so atrocious a demand. For what he did do I was as utterly unprepared as anybody present. Remember that during all this conversation they had never loosed the cords which bound our wrists; so you may imagine the wild astonishment with which I saw my father, having taken a step forward as if to put his foot upon the crucifix, suddenly disengage his hands as if by magic, strike the little commander a tremendous blow in the face which promptly knocked him flat on his back, and then jump over his prostrate body and disappear into the forest close behind him!

The whole thing was so sudden, so startling, so comical that, in spite of the still formidable circumstances, I burst into a peal of laughter, which was echoed by little Gerald. All was confusion for a few moments. The officers rushed to pick up their half-stunned commander, and fetched a camp-stool for him to sit upon. The men in the camp behind shouted with surprise and, though I am not actually sure of it, I have a strong suspicion that my laugh was echoed by some of them also. In the few moments while Martinez was recovering, no one seemed to know exactly what to do. Possibly the second in command was not on the spot, but at any rate nothing was done, and I suppose that it may have been five minutes before the commander, after much drinking of water and much gasping and swearing under his breath, was once more in a condition to speak.

When he found utterance his language was not parliamentary. He was purple and choking with rage. He dragged himself to his feet, though at first he could stand only by leaning with his hand upon the table. He drew his sword; he flourished it, and the looks which he cast upon his officers were so savage that it really seemed as though he was going to use it.

" Where is that scoundrel? " he shouted.

The officers looked at one another with stupefaction, for up to that moment I verily believe that no one had thought of pursuing the fugitive. Martinez became madder than ever.

" What! " he roared, " you have let him escape! imbeciles! incapables! pursue him at once—at once, I tell you! My honour has been insulted, and I will have his blood."

Hurriedly some arrangements were made for the pursuit, and one or two companies of soldiers were hastily marshalled and sent off to beat the forest. As soon as they had departed Martinez turned his rage upon me. He seemed to be almost foaming at the mouth, and looked as though he was possessed by a devil, and he hissed his words between his teeth as though he were on the point of literal physical explosion.

"Son of a scoundrel!" he said, "within an hour you shall see your villain father hanged on that tree!"

"You will have to catch him first", I interrupted, with a laugh—which was not politic, I admit. But I was so glad to see my father escape that I did not think of that then, nor of the fact that, if *he* had escaped, I certainly had not.

"You impudent young dog!" he spluttered. (I really cannot translate the exact phrase which he used, but it was worse than that.) "You at least shall swear allegiance, and you had better do it at once, or I will have you flayed alive."

I am afraid I laughed again, which was rude of me, but he really did look so utterly ridiculous in his impotent rage, and with a great lump already rising between his eyes, where my father had struck him.

"I shall do no such thing," I said; "and if you dare to touch me, my father will repay you for it when he comes back."

He half raised his sword, and for a moment it looked very much as though my career would be cut short then and there. But somehow he controlled himself, and an evil glint came into his one available eye (the other was fast closing under the influence of the blow). He turned and called Antinahuel.

" Perhaps," he said, " your men can manage to make this young coxcomb change his mind. Don't you think so? "

A slight disdainful smile passed over Antinahuel's face.

" Perhaps they may ", and he signed to some of his men, who came up and began to drag me away. Martinez said no further words to him, but turned upon my little brother Gerald.

" You, at least, you little spawn of the devil, put your foot on that cross and repeat after me the words which I shall say to you."

" Don't you do it. Gerald," I shouted back to him, as I was being dragged off; " remember S. Agnes! "

For not long before we had left home, our mother had told us the legend of S. Agnes, a Roman maiden of thirteen, who, it was alleged, had died for the sake of her faith sooner than perform some act of sacrifice which was against her conscience. Or perhaps she refused to be betrothed to what she called a heathen—I am not quite sure after all these years. But I know that the story had recently been told to us, and that we had both greatly admired the little girl's heroism.

I wrenched myself free sufficiently to look back and see what the little boy did. He looked up quite bravely into the furious face of Martinez, and said in his clear childish treble:

"I will not do it. You are a very wicked man."

What followed next I do not like to tell, even though I really believe now in my inmost heart that it was the act of a madman. Martinez whirled his sword above his head and cut the child down as he stood looking up in his face. When he saw the little body lying before him I think even he was ashamed, for he threw down his sword and turned away, muttering something about not having meant to do it. Even his officers, a set of hardened ruffians, showed some disgust on their faces, and all drew back as Martinez walked hurriedly into his tent.

What this meant to me, who loved that little brother more than my own life, I can hardly tell you. What I did I cannot justify; I can only tell you that I also was half mad with grief and rage. But then and there I, a captive in the hands of ruthless savages, and little likely, so far as could be seen, to live to see to-morrow's sun, registered with all the force of burning hate a solemn vow that I would never turn aside from the pursuit until I had slain Martinez in revenge for the death of my brother. I was wrong, of course, but I was only a young boy and the provocation was terrible.

Meantime I soon had my own affairs to think of. The Indians dragged me away to the borders of the forest, and after a little searching they found what they wanted—two young and flexible trees growing only a few yards apart. Four or five threw themselves upon each tree, and by their united weight and strength bent down the tops until they came almost together, and then they proceeded to tie me between these two tops, the right arm and leg to one, the left arm and leg to the other; and as soon as that was done to their satisfaction the men let go the trees, which instantly sprang back as far as they could and left me hanging between them. A diabolically ingenious woodsman's substitute for the mediæval rack of the Inquisition.

To be left hanging in such a position for hours under such a nerve-rending strain is an experience which I would rather not try to describe; nor need I tell in detail how they stood jeering underneath as I hung in mid air as though on an invisible S. Andrew's cross. Nor how they pelted my aching body with fragments of broken bottles, or struck at me from beneath with long lianas, torn from the neighbouring trees. I will not harrow your feelings with a description of the unnamable tortures which they inflicted upon me all through that weary day.

But this at least I can say, that however horrible were the sufferings all through the day, only the one overpowering feeling burned ever stronger and stronger within my heart and mind—black, bitter hatred of Martinez, and the resolve to be revenged upon him for my brother's death. So entirely was I wrapped up in this that I believe for the most part I gave no answer to their repeated enquiries whether I would not now take the required oath. But I know that sometimes I replied by calling down curses upon their heads and threatening that dire vengeance should overtake them. It is best to draw a veil over this. Let me say only that their ingenuity was diabolical and their resources seemed endless.

I suppose that they got tired of me at last, as I showed no signs of yielding to them, and they felt that they must do something to bring matters to a crisis. So they hung me from the branch of a tree by a rope passed under my shoulders, and then proceeded to light a fire beneath my feet, which were soon most horribly burnt. But at the same time the hot air and the smoke half suffocated me, and evidently I must have fainted. I suppose this frightened them, for their orders were not to kill me; and so for that night they desisted from their cruel work. But of all this I know nothing.

CHAPTER IV

THE FLIGHT

I REGAINED consciousness only slowly and confusedly, coming back into a strange and terrible sense of all-pervading pain, which seemed to fill the whole world. Gradually this world of acute anguish contracted and became more definite, until at last I realized myself as a small boy still alive upon the physical plane and in a condition of horrible suffering. I found myself bound to a tree, just at the borders of the forest, not far from the tent of Martinez—bound by a rope which passed round me and the tree many times, and so formed a support without which I must of course have fallen, as the soles of my feet were so shockingly burnt that it would have been quite impossible for me to stand upon them for a moment.

It was night, and the camp lay quiet before me, except for the sentinels who walked steadily up and down on their beats. Two of these were not far from me, one passing up and down in front of the commander's tent, and the other taking a much

15

longer beat along a certain section just outside of the nearest row of tents. No one seemed to be specially guarding me; indeed it was quite unnecessary, as I was not only securely tied, but I could not have moved a yard even if I had been free.

As may easily be imagined, my thoughts were of the saddest. My brother had been murdered before my eyes; my father was a fugitive in a trackless forest, which I knew to be full of wild beasts, and was further-more being pursued relentlessly by men who knew no mercy. I had nothing to expect but certain death—probably of the most appallingly painful kind. So perhaps I need not be ashamed to acknowledge that for a time I felt absolutely despairing, and only wished that death might come even now to release me from further suffering. The conditions were so bad in every way that it seemed to me that they could not be worse, and I actually even prayed for death, saying that I could bear no more.

But just at this moment of utter weakness and despondency, I saw something which for the moment actually made me forget even that excruciating pain; for there, just in front of me, stood my brother Gerald, whom I had seen only a few hours before cut down by the sword of Martinez! Indeed, the mark of that cruel blow still lay across his head —a great ghastly wound cleaving the skull asunder.

And yet somehow even that did not look terrible at all, for the expression of the face was so sweet that it quite overpowered the impression given by the wound. He stood before me exactly as in life the flickering light of distant campfires fully upon him, and yet his form seemed also to be surrounded by a faint light of its own.

But the wonderful thing was the expression of the face. It was the same child-face I knew so well, changed in no particular, and yet showing so much more than it had ever shown before. That he himself was happy—radiantly happy, and utterly at peace—no one could have doubted for a moment; and yet the eyes were filled with pity (but pity obviously for me only, and not at all for himself) and with the desire to encourage and strengthen me. I tried to speak, but could not; nor did he on his side say a word; but he took a step forward, his face broke out into a radiant smile of love, and he laid his hand caressingly upon my breast. And then, in a moment, he was gone, just before the sentinel, who had reached the end of his beat, turned his face in our direction once more.

I find it difficult to describe the effect which this beautiful little apparition had upon me. All my manifold pains were still as insistent as ever—my whole body was still nothing but one mass of agony;

and yet my mental attitude had in that moment become just the reverse of what it had been before. Remember that I knew nothing then of the astral world, nothing of the possibilities of life after death; so to me this was a special portent from heaven, a special sign from God Himself, who had permitted my brother's spirit to return from the unseen world in order to cheer and comfort me in my trouble.

Inevitably then followed the certainty that, however hopeless the prospect might appear, somehow or other all would be well. Either, impossible as it appeared, I should somehow escape and recover, or else, if I was to die, I knew that I should die soon and painlessly, and be with my brother once more. Since outward circumstances were entirely unchanged, it is perhaps hard to comprehend that my despondency had vanished as though it had never been, and that I was now in a condition of eager expectancy—expectancy that something would happen, either death or some kind of liberation. What form this latter would take I could not imagine, and I remember reviewing the situation without being able to find a single reasonable suggestion.

If I remember rightly, I think I had decided that if there was to be some kind of intervention, the most likely form for it to take was that in some unexpected way the Government might have received warning of the forced marches which Martinez supposed to be unknown to them, and that they on their part might have sent a force to intercept and surround him. I knew that that was practically impossible, yet every other supposition seemed even more impossible still, unless I was to expect some sort of direct angelic intervention, and I knew that such things were rare in these latter days. But that something would happen either to kill me or to release me I felt quite assured. And when the something *did* happen, although it came in a way which had never for a moment occurred to me, it was only for the moment that I was startled.

I felt the touch of a hand, evidently extended from behind the tree, and immediately afterwards I was conscious that the rope which bound me with such painful tightness to the tree was relaxing. I remember it flashed through my mind that my unknown friend behind the tree was probably not aware that I was unable to stand, and should certainly fall as soon as that rope was removed, and that thus his amiable intentions would be frustrated, and the sentry's attention attracted. But that was evidently foreseen. My deliverer waited until the nearest sentry's back was turned, and then, as the rope slackened, an arm came round, caught me and drew me quickly and silently behind the tree. I had just time to recognize in the faint flash of the distant firelight that my rescuers were my father and the Negro servant Tito, when the latter picked me up in his arms, and we executed a hurried and silent retreat into the forest.

When we had penetrated perhaps two hundred yards Tito laid me down, pulled out his huge clasp-knife and quickly cut the cords which still bound my wrists; but even when my arms were free I was unable to use them, because they had been so cramped and strained by the many hours of confinement. We exchanged a few hurried words, my father commiserating me for my sufferings, and I interrupting to ask whether he knew of Gerald's fate, and in the same breath assuring him that I had seen him since his death. My father seemed hardly to understand; I think that he supposed me to be delirious—as indeed I well might have been, considering all that I had been through; at any rate he said that he knew of Gerald's death, and that we must not stop to talk now, but must make every effort to get as far away from the camp as possible before my escape should be discovered. I was a helpless burden upon them, as I could not walk a step, and even the motion of being carried, gently and carefully as Tito did it, cost me harrowing pain.

In the dense forest the darkness was intense, and it was necessary that we should move as silently as possible, and with the utmost circumspection; so our advance was naturally of the slowest. Every moment we expected that an alarm would be given, and that we should hear the commencement of a pursuit. But I hoped that the sentry might not notice my absence, because the tree to which I had been bound was at some distance from him, just within the shade at the edge of the wood, and the campfires, which, an hour or two earlier had lit up that place, were now dying down. Time went on and nothing happened, and we made such progress as we could, but even at the best it was painfully slow. I knew nothing of the direction in which we were going, for the only thing of which we thought was to put as great a distance as possible between ourselves and that camp. Soon we found that the ground was rising—in places rather steeply.

All too soon for us the dawn came, and the earth leaped from dark night into broad daylight with the suddenness peculiar to the tropics. At the first light Tito laid me gently down, and asked my father to sit with me while he looked round for some place of concealment, as it was clear that we were still far too near the camp to avoid discovery unless we contrived to hide ourselves. Also it seems that I was rapidly sinking into stupor of exhaustion, and Tito, who knew something about medicine as practised among the Negroes, thought it would be dangerous for me to push on further.

After some search he found a place that would suit us admirably, and came back to carry me to it. It was a huge tree of unknown age, the heart of which had gradually rotted away, so that there was quite a chamber inside it, carpeted deeply by a soft powdering of decayed wood—a kind of natural sawdust. To all appearance the tree was as perfect and sound as those around it, and the only way to enter this sylvan chamber was by climbing up the tree to a height of some fifteen feet, and then lowering oneself through a hole, whence perhaps a branch had fallen a century ago. The problem was how to get me into this retreat; but it was a case of necessity, and at last the thing was accomplished.

My father slipped off the poncho which had been given to him the day before. I was laid on that, and the corners were tied together so as to make a kind of cradle. Through that Tito slipped the rope which had bound me to the tree, which he had had the forethought to bring with him, rightly thinking that in our desperate condition almost anything might come in useful. Then he climbed the tree to a certain height, my father throwing up the end of the rope to him, and slowly and with great care he raised me from the ground and got me wedged between the trunk of the tree and a huge liana. Then he descended and helped my father to mount, and left him to hold on precariously to the liana and to support me, while he himself climbed a little higher, obtained a foothold close to the hole, and then by means of the rope drew me up and rested me beside him. Then he dropped lightly down upon the dust, which made that inside floor much higher than the level of the ground outside. My father then climbed up the few remaining feet, and carefully lowered me down into the arms of Tito. Soon they had me laid upon the floor, and it seemed almost comfortable to be able thus to rest in a recumbent position after so many hours of misery.

I hoped to sleep, but fever had seized upon me, and I believe that most of that day I was barely conscious, and at times even delirious. I knew nothing of what was going forward, but my father told me afterwards that, almost as soon as we were established, they heard a great noise from the direction of the camp, and an amount of shouting which evidently betokened great excitement. The faithful Tito climbed to the top of our tree and found that, because of the rising ground, he was able to see most of the camp. He reported much hurry and tumult, and presently declared that large bodies of soldiers were being sent into the forest in several different directions, evidently to search for us.

You see, our recapture was of enormous importance to the plans of Martinez. He had succeeded in altogether eluding the Government forces which had been sent out in pursuit of him. By several days of almost incredible forced marching he had contrived to lead his men into a position from which they could easily attack a town of great importance. His manœuvre was entirely unexpected by the Government army whom he had deluded into the idea that he had moved in the opposite direction; indeed, they were occupied in hunting down the small band which he had sent down there in order to mislead them—they supposing that that was his entire army. He had halted his men at the spot where we had made his acquaintance, to give them a couple of days' rest after the forced marching before they swept down upon the town, and in that wild district it was reasonably certain that he could not have been seen or his presence reported.

But if I and my father, or even one of us alone, could escape, could by some incredible means make his way to the nearest house or village, and thence send the alarm down to the seaport city, all Martinez's advantage would be lost; and since he had risked everything on this one bold move we may say that his cause would be lost too, and his life unquestionably forfeited. Therefore it was of capital importance for him to get hold of us at all costs, and so, instead of allowing his men to rest as he had intended them to do, he sent them out to range the forest in search of us. He knew well that we could not have gone far, for he knew that I at least was sorely wounded, and that my father had no weapon; nor can it have seemed conceivable to him that we could escape for a single day the myriad dangers that surrounded us on every side in that forest. He did not know that we had the invaluable assistance of Tito, who knew all about these things, and was perfectly capable of protecting himself in the forest, and of wringing subsistence out of it.

They told me that groups of soldiers again and again came past the very tree in which we were hiding. They even overheard scraps of their conversation, and Tito, who knew their language perfectly, reported that they spoke much of witchcraft and of a supernatural deliverance. It was evident from what they said that the superstitions of Martinez also had been aroused, and that he was in a condition of panic fear. He thought (it seems one of his officers had told him so) that in killing Gerald he had brought ill-luck upon himself; he was unable to understand, as indeed were all of them, how my father could suddenly have got free when he was obviously securely bound, and he thought of my disappearance when I was practically at the point of death, as another instance of supernatural interference.

I remember that my father said that at one time some soldiers had thrown themselves down to rest quite close to the tree. Tito listened eagerly to their conversation, anxious to pick up any information that might be of use to us; and my father was oppressed with the fear that I might reveal our hiding-place by giving vent to low delirious mutterings. Fortunately this did not happen, and in the course of the afternoon I fell into a deep refreshing sleep, from which they wakened me only when darkness had fallen, and it was time to set out once more.

Meantime Tito had risked his life by climbing out of our refuge more than once to fetch some water for me, and some leaves of a plant which he knew, which he chewed into a paste and laid upon my burnt feet and some of the worst of my wounds. I do not know what this remedy was, but its effect was magical in the relief of pain, for when I was awakened in the evening, though still weak and in great suffering, I was distinctly much better than in the morning, and all traces of fever had for the time left me. The soldiers had retired to their camp just before nightfall, but we had little doubt from what had been overheard that the search would be renewed the next day. I felt great regret at leaving my soft couch, and in truth somewhat doubted the wisdom of moving on at all, since we had discovered so excellent a shelter; but both Tito and my father felt that they would know no ease until they were much further away from the camp.

They got me out of our refuge much in the same way as they had before got me in, and we set off up the hill. The whole general trend of the ground seemed to be upward, and several times during the night we came to little open places from which we were able to see the campfires of our enemies far below us. As we rose higher the trees grew somewhat less thickly, and our progress was on the whole rather more rapid—less slow would be a better way to put it. Once again dawn came, and Tito searched for a hiding-place, but this time no convenient hollow tree was to be found. We were in a region of magnificent monarchs of the forest, mostly with wide spaces between them, but so huge were they that though their trunks might be a hundred feet or even two hundred feet apart, their branches often intermingled high above our heads. These giants would have been quite unclimbable except for the fact that in nearly every case huge lianas, with trunks as large as many a tree in these cold northern climes, wreathed round their splendid trunks and usually afforded a comparatively easy way of ascent for an active person.

While Tito was ranging about in search of a hiding-place it occurred to him to climb one of these great trees in order to see what our enemies were doing. Without much trouble he found a place from which the camp was still clearly visible, though very minute now in the far distance, and he saw the same hurry and preparation and sending out of troops as before; but though he saw nothing new he presently heard something which sent him down the tree at his best speed, and he came rushing to us, with a face of that curious livid grey which is the nearest that a Negro can come to turning white with fear.

"Dogs, master!" he said, "they are setting the slave-dogs on us. Listen!"

When we listened attentively, sure enough we heard far off the sonorous bay of a bloodhound. We knew that these great dogs were kept by certain slave-owners in the interior to track down runaway Negroes; but how Martinez could have got hold of one we could not imagine. I can only suppose that among his men there must have been one who knew of the existence of such creatures on some inland plantation, that he must have mentioned the matter to his officer, and that when Martinez heard of it he must at once have sent off some men to borrow these dogs, even though to do so would put the great secret of his presence there into the hands of some at least of the people of that plantation. Indeed I fear much, knowing something of his character, that he may have adopted terribly efficacious means to ensure the silence of every human being upon that plantation; perhaps there may have been a wholesale massacre.

At any rate there were the dogs, and there could be little doubt of their ability to track us, both to our hiding-place of the day before and to the place where we now were, and our chance of escaping them seemed remarkably small. I had often heard stories of the untamable ferocity of these creatures, and of their resolution in following up a trail to the last. We sought no more for a place of conceal-ment, but hurried hopelessly on, tending ever up-wards towards the summit of the mountains. But we knew well that the progress of our pursuers would be very much faster than our own, and that nothing could save us from being overtaken.

Tito had a theory, founded upon some Negro superstition, that the smell of blood would destroy the keenness of scent of the hounds, so he drew out his big knife and made with it a slight cut in his arm, sprinkling the blood which flowed plentifully around the spot where we were then standing. He seemed to have some confidence in this method, although he admitted that with some dogs it had been known to fail; so it seemed rather a slender reed to support the edifice of our hopes. We were at this time on the edge of a sort of ridge, and in front of us the ground dipped again, and made a kind of ravine, along the bottom of which flowed a shallow stream. On the other side of the stream the ground rose again, and the hillside stretched on before us. Looking at this stream a flash of inspiration came to me, as my father held me in his arms.

"Father," I said excitedly, "don't you remember the histoy of Scotland? Don't you remember how Robert Bruce was once pursued by bloodhounds, and how he escaped from them by walking in the water, so that he left no trail?"

A light of hope appeared in my father's eye. "Why, yes," he said, "I have heard that story, long ago when I was at school. At least we can try it."

Rapidly he explained the method to Tito, who at first seemed hardly to comprehend, but as the idea penetrated he said:

"That is true. Of course scent will not lie in the water. But then we cannot lie in the river, and when we get out again the dogs will smell us."

"No, Tito," said I, "walk along the river until you find a big branch hanging over it, and then pull yourself out by the branch without touching the ground."

"That is it," said my father; "let us try it. It may succeed, and anyhow there is nothing else to do."

I think Tito was doubtful about it, for he had a well-founded terror of those awful dogs; but we hurried down into the ravine, into the shallow stream, and then began to wade steadily up it.

They had to walk some distance (I cannot say we, for I was being carried all the time, and was acutely sensible how much I added to the dangers of the party) before we could find in the right position a branch which Tito thought possible. But even then, he took us on past two or three which might have suited us, because they belonged to giant trees which stood all alone, and he wished to have a line of retreat open to him.

Meantime the baying of the dogs sounded alarmingly near; but at last we came to a branch which satisfied Tito's fastidiousness, because it belonged to a tree whose branches interlocked with others, so that it might be possible for us to make our way (as the monkeys do) along what may be called the upper storey of the forest. The branch was thick and strong, but just beyond reach by jumping, and here arose a difficulty. The streamlet was but knee-deep, and it was easy enough for us to wade in it, but if my father should lay me down upon the bank a clue would be given to those remorseless brutes who were following us so closely.

They did not want to lay me down in the water —as they might easily have done, for I could have sat with my head above its surface—because the paste of leaves which Tito had made was still covering my wounded feet, and he declared that inflammation might set in if it were removed; so my poor

16

father had to stand holding my heavy weight in his arms while Tito climbed cautiously up him and stood upon his shoulders. Then, with a very little jump he was able to grasp the branch and to pull himself up upon it. Then, unwinding the rope (which he had carried round his waist) he soon had me up beside him and carried me a little w..y to where a fork gave a place in which he could safely leave me, while he went back and pulled up my father by means of the same rope.

We found ourselves upon a branch as large as the trunk of many a tree, so that they were able to walk along it quite easily towards the giant trunk, supporting themselves by the many branchlets which sprang from it and by the twisted lianas which were hanging all around us. They were soon at the trunk and, crawling round it, made their way along a branch at the opposite side. Then, stepping off from that to an equally huge branch of another tree, which interpenetrated this one, they were able to follow that up to its trunk and to pass from that tree into a third, so that we we were now at a considerable distance from the stream, and high up the hill.

Climbing a little further up this third tree, Tito discovered a place where two branches, leaving the trunk side by side, provided a comfortable platform on which there was plenty of room for us all; on which also I could be laid out—not quite so softly, perhaps, as in the tree-trunk of the previous day, but still with some degree of comfort. We got ourselves settled there only just in time. We were high enough up the tree to enable us to see over the ridge, and soon a party of soldiers came into sight, with two bloodhounds in front, each held in a leash, and eagerly straining forward. They came up to the spot where poor Tito had so unnecessarily shed his blood, but it had no appreciable effect in checking them. They smelt about for a moment, and uttered savage bays, I suppose at the smell of the blood. But they resumed the trail immediately, and followed it over the edge of the ridge and down to the water. There they stopped, but the soldiers waded in and encouraged them to cross. When they reached the other side, however, they halted and appeared to be at a loss. The soldiers said:

"They have turned up or down."

The company immediately divided, each party taking a dog with them, one going up the river and the other down. Those who turned upwards presently came to the tree by which we had pulled ourselves out of the water, but the dog gave no sign, and the soldiers passed on. After a time they came back again on the other side of the stream, it apparently having occurred to them that we might not have crossed it after all. Then, on returning on the trail, they began to shout to the others, who had gone downwards, and then sent a man running after them, and soon we saw that party also returning on the other side of the water. Then a consultation was held, and it was evident that they did not know what to do next.

Presently the officers in charge gave an order, and the men dispersed—evidently to search the neighbourhood; but it seemed to me that they went off very slowly and unwillingly. Some of them passed close underneath our tree, and once more we heard them talking about witchcraft, and declaring that it was useless to search for us, as the devil had evidently carried us off because we were heretics—which struck me as rather amusing on the part of men who had, at least for the time, openly renounced the Christian religion themselves, and practically bound themselves to worship only that fiend Martinez. They spoke also of the anger of Martinez, and his wild asseverations that at all costs we must be recaptured; they suggested that he was mad with terror, and indeed I think he may have been.

It seemed impossible that the idea that we must be hiding in a tree should not occur to them; yet apparently it did not. I believe that, if they had had the sense to bring some of the Indians with them, our little ruse would have been penetrated;

but fortunately for us there was a good deal of jealousy and ill-feeling between these allies, and so Martinez had evidently determined to do the work with his own men. All day the soldiers patrolled up and down at intervals, evidently driven by their officer to keep moving, yet fully convinced that their task was a hopeless one, and continuing to pursue it half-heartedly only for the sake of being able to say that they had done something. At different times we caught scraps of conversation, but always to much the same effect—dread of the anger of Martinez, speculation as to what he would do, and suggestions and stories of the supernatural.

The day wore slowly on, and this time Tito dared not leave our post even for a moment, for the slightest motion of the leaves might possibly attract attention, with so many searchers wandering about eager to gain the reward which (we heard them say) Martinez had promised to anyone who should find us. The day before he had brought in a bunch or two of wild fruit, but to-day we could get nothing whatever, and both he and my father were suffering much from the pangs of hunger, for it was now nearly three days since they had had anything worth speaking of to eat. I myself was probably better without food for a while in my condition of weakness, though now that I was somewhat better from the fever I had begun to feel some hunger. I suffered more from lack of water, for the fever returned slightly during the day; but there was nothing for it but to be still and take care not to show ourselves.

When the sun was nearing the horizon, the officer gathered his party together and they departed down the hill, taking their dogs with them; but we could clearly detect the reluctance which they felt to go back and face the anger of Martinez with the report of failure. Fearing the possibility of some trick, we watched them well on their way before we ventured to leave our hiding-place, and then Tito hurried down to reconnoitre, and search for some food before darkness actually fell. He was fortunately successful in finding some guavas and wild bananas, and a little later some bread-fruit, and presently he dug up for us some kind of tubers which had a faintly sweet flavour.

I could take but little of these, but my father and Tito made a meal which, though hardly satis-factory, was at least a great improvement on the scanty fare of the previous day.

I was lowered carefully out of the tree, and we resumed our flight. When morning came again, we were on the shoulder of the mountain, and Tito once more climbed the highest tree in sight, in hope of gaining some information with regard to the movements of the soldiers. He was unable to see the camp, but after listening with the utmost care he came down convinced that we were not immediately menaced in any way—certainly not by the dogs, whose cries would have been audible for a long distance in the calm morning air. Under these circumstances Tito advised continuing our flight for some time by day, and this was accordingly done. They pushed on, still beneath the shade of the trees, but now in a downward direction, until about eleven o'clock, when they decided to make a halt at the side of a tiny stream of water. My father and I lay down to sleep while Tito watched. As he saw nothing whatever that seemed in the least suspicious, he lay down to sleep in his turn, when my father woke an hour later.

At this time Tito ventured gently to wash off his paste of leaves and examine my wounds, because he was now able to get some more leaves of the same kind, with which he replaced his previous dressing. He reported that they were all doing well—that is to say, as well as could be expected—even the feet; though I overheard him, when he thought he was out of ear-shot of me, expressing his doubts to my father as to whether I should ever really be able to walk again. On this day also for the first time we were able to talk in comfort, and I had the opportunity of hearing my father's story.

The explanation of the apparent miracle of his escape was in reality exceedingly simple. It appears that the Indians had made the mistake of tying his hands with a green raw-hide rope, and during the long night ride through the forest he had set himself by steady pressure gradually to stretch this as much as he could, until finally he could slip his hand through it. He was wise enough, however, not to let our Indian captors see this, and by straining slightly against it he easily contrived to give the notion that he was still tightly bound.

But he was all the time awaiting his opportunity, and when he saw the arrangement of Martinez's tent, and that the forest was so close behind it, it occurred to him that here was an opportunity of escape of which a bold man who moved with lightning rapidity might easily take advantage. He realized that he was for the moment abandoning his sons, and so he did not take the step until it was quite evident that Martinez could not be moved from his position. He said that he scarcely expected to be allowed even so much as a minute before the pursuit commenced, and that he regarded the whole affair as the most desperate of chances; but still there seemed to be literally nothing else to be done, and as this was the only way, he took it.

As I have said, the whole thing was so unexpected, and the consequent confusion so great, that he really got five minutes' start, and made good use of it. He knew that he could not hope by mere running to tire out men who had horses at their disposal, so from the first as he ran he sought for a place to hide in. The pursuit had often come quite close to him, and he had been on the brink of discovery half a dozen times; somehow he just contrived to dodge his pursuers, and after a time the idea of tree-climbing was suggested to him by the fact that the various monkeys whom he startled as he moved from place to place invariably took at once to the trees, and as invariably vanished utterly from sight, even when he was only a few yards from them.

"If they can do this," he thought, "surely a man can do it also."

So before the searching soldiers came back again, he had already found himself a nest in one of the larger trees. When the soldiers had passed for the second time, and he thought he was safe for the moment, he was much alarmed to see a Negro moving stealthily through the forest, evidently searching for something—for *him*, he greatly feared.

Indeed, this proved to be the case, for this was the faithful Tito, who had been aware of the attack upon the cabin, but had been cut off from return to it by the cordon of besieging Indians. He had lurked in the neighbourhood in the hope of being able to render some assistance to his master, had seen the capture and had run through the whole night on the track of the party. He had concealed himself in the edge of the forest, had witnessed his master's escape and Gerald's death, and had also seen something of what had happened to me. He was afraid to rejoin his master while the soldiers were still in the woods, as they had established a sort of central meeting-point, at which their various parties reported progress, quite close to the tree which he had selected for his hiding-place.

As soon as the soldiers had finally withdrawn he descended, and began to quarter that part of the forest in search of his master, and though he did not actually find him, he came in sight of him, and as soon as my father was assured of his identity he called to him. Their joy at meeting was tempered by the dreadful news as to Gerald which Tito had to convey. Then they consulted as to what could be done, and decided that, heart-rending as it was, they could do nothing whatever during the day-time, but if I survived until the evening they cherished some hope of being able during the night to effect a rescue—as in fact they did.

Of course I told my story of the apparition of my brother, and Tito, I am sure, fully believed it, for he said:

" Master Gerald sure was an angel when he was on earth, and sure he is an angel now; and the good God sends His angels to help those who are suffering." My father was not so certain; all that he would permit himself was:

"Well, my boy, I do not know what to say; they do say that God sometimes allows the dead to return for His own good purposes, and of course there is the story of Samuel and the witch of Endor; and we hear too that some of the Saints have shown themselves. Anyhow, whether Gerald himself was there or not, we are surely right in saying that it was God who sent the vision to comfort you, for it came just at the right time, and it gave you the courage to endure until we came to rescue you."

I need not tell in detail the further story of our flight. From that time on we travelled by day and rested by night, my father and Tito each watching in turn. We gradually worked our way down the other side of our mountain and round its base, advancing then with the greatest circumspection, lest we should fall foul of Martinez and his army; but fortunately we saw nothing of them, and we contrived each day to get something in the way of food, though it was only fruit and roots.

My great sorrow was that I must all the time be such a burden upon the others, because I was quite incapable of walking even a step, and this made our progress so slow. It may be that the frugal diet and the life in the open air was in reality the best thing for the cure of my wounds. Tito did well enough, but my father, who had had a touch of consumption in England, suffered from the changes in temperature and the lack of the clothing to which he was accustomed; for he had nothing but the dirty old poncho which had been given to him—now no longer dirty, for Tito had washed it thoroughly in a mountain stream. Tito was little better off, for he had only the shirt and light cotton trousers which he was wearing at the time of the attack; and I was distinctly worse off, for I had absolutely nothing at all!

I think it was on the eleventh day that, from some rising ground, we at last caught sight of the roof of a house. Promptly we made our way in that direction, and then my father and I hid ourselves, while Tito went ahead to reconnoitre. He found the place to be a *hacienda* or country-house, and as soon as he came into the presence of the owner and told his story to him, the good gentleman immediately manifested the greatest concern, and came hurrying out with Tito to see what could be done for us.

From that moment our troubles were over. Our worthy friend and his most kindly wife treated us with the utmost hospitality. The good lady was full of pity for my condition, though I was now far on the road to recovery, and insisted on my going to bed and having my feet dressed and bandaged in somewhat less primitive fashion. Loud were their denunciations of the inhumanity of Martinez, when my story came to be told in detail. Our host, who, like so many others of the *haciendados*, lived on entirely secluded life on his own estates through the greater part of each year, had known nothing whatever of the presence of Martinez in his neighbourhood. Once in two months or so he usually sent his servant, or more usually a party of two or three servants, down to the seaport town, to bring his letters if there were any, and to purchase such stores as he could not provide on his own estate.

We had no idea as to what might have been happening during the days of our flight, and we rather feared that Martinez might have succeeded in taking the city unawares, so our host called together his servants and told them the news which we had brought, and asked for volunteers to go down to the coast and discover the condition of affairs. Several of his men immediately offered themselves for the service, and out of these he chose two young fellows, explaining that he did not wish to send more because it was impossible to say that the *hacienda* itself might not be attacked during their absence, and he desired to keep as large a garrison as he could. These two young men were then sent off upon their journey, with many charges to exercise the utmost vigilance, and even when they reached the town on no account to ride straight into it as was usual, lest they should find it in the occupation of the insurgents.

Our host told us that, if no accident happened to them, they might well be back in a week, and that the only thing we could do was to spend the intervening time with him; though he hoped indeed that, if the news which came to us was good, we would consent to honour his poor roof by a much longer stay. We thanked him heartily for his hospitable intent, but told him that as soon as possible we must get back to my mother, so that she might know that at least she was not deprived of both her sons and her husband. My father, indeed, had confided a letter for her to the care of the two messengers, telling her in outline what had happened, and that we two were now safe, and in the best of hands. Our host also had entrusted to them a letter to a friend of his, who was a high official in the town, telling him of the presence of Martinez and warning him to see at once to the defence of the town, if it were not already too late.

During that pleasant week we, to a great extent, recovered ourselves. The cough which had been troubling my father grew better, though indeed he never was quite free from it, and he finally died of consumption in England a few years later. I always felt that but for the villainous Martinez, and the exposure which he had forced upon us by his proceedings, my father might have survived for many years more. For myself, I seemed for the time to have lost my boyhood. I was unable to move about, but after all I did not want to do so, and I seemed to desire only to rest. Much of the time I spent in bed, though for some part of each day they always carried me down into the great sitting-room where I was generally laid upon a sort of settee, or sometimes they carried me out into the garden and put me in a long wicker-work chair under the trees.

I did not know whether to be glad or sorry when at last the messengers came back, bringing the reassuring news that the city knew nothing whatever of Martinez and of his movements. Our host's official friend had sent him a party of twenty soldiers to garrison the *hacienda* if it should be attacked, and meantime thanked him heartily for his warning, and stated that the city had been hastily put in a thorough state of defence, and that scouts had been sent into the interior to try to discover Martinez and his little army.

Our host and hostess pressed us urgently to stay with them until the attack was over and Martinez was defeated, for they felt quite sure that this would be the outcome of the struggle. My father felt, however, that it was his duty to be by his wife's side, and so, with many heartfelt thanks, he declined this kindly offer. Our friend had a palanquin constructed for me, and offered to send back with us to the coast the same two young men who had already once made the journey. Then he pressed us also to take with us half the band of soldiers as an escort. My father would by no means consent to this, as he felt that while we were still uncertain as to the position of Martinez the *hacienda* might be attacked, and every man would be necessary for its defence; but he gladly accepted the offer of the two young servants to carry the litter, promising them a large reward when he should safely reach the coast.

Our host insisted about the soldiers, and eventually we had to compromise by allowing three of them to accompany us, and indeed they proved themselves both merry companions and very useful fellows, constantly relieving the servants in the carrying of the litter when they where tired, and so enabling us to make fairly constant progress instead of having to rest at least half of the time, as would otherwise have been the case. One of them, who was a clever man with his hands, contrived a scheme by means of which the litter could be slung between two horses, so that when we came to a long stretch of level ground we could make much easier and more rapid progress. In this way we journeyed along, meeting with no special adventures, and we finally reached our home on the sixth day from that on which we left the *hacienda*.

The mother met us, mourning deeply indeed for her lost son, yet devoutly thankful after such wild experiences to welcome her surviving son and her husband—safe at any rate, if not exactly sound. It was six weeks from the night of our escape from Martinez before I was able to set my feet to the ground, and even then for a long time I had to walk warily and but little at a time.

Exactly what had happened to Martinez and his plans we never clearly understood. My mother always believed that, because of the wicked murder of my brother, some sort of divine curse had fallen upon him, so that he was no longer capable of decisive action. My father was more disposed to think that our escape had disheartened him, because he supposed that we should certainly be able to convey to the coast town the warning of his presence, and so defeat his plan. Much later, vague rumours were afloat of disaffection among his followers, of rebellions against his cruelty, and of a general opinion among his men that his dash

17

and good fortune had left him. However all this may be, the fact remains that that attack upon the seaport town was never delivered, and that Martinez instead disappeared into the interior with his followers, and that no authentic news was received of him for nearly three months.

Then came the tidings that he had attacked a small town away in the interior, and had occupied and fortified it, having killed all such of its inhabitants as refused to swear. allegiance to him. As soon as this story was confirmed, all was activity in military circles. Such regiments as were available were got together and put on a war footing, and the Council of the town issued a call for volunteers, since the number of soldiers was but few, and they were very anxious that there should be not the slightest doubt as to the assembling of a sufficient force definitely to crush Martinez.

My father, though fretting much at the delay with regard to his railway, had made no attempt to engage any body of workmen, saying that he would be no party to the risking of any men's lives away there in the jungle, until both Martinez and his Indian allies were finally disposed of in some way. As soon as he heard of the formation of the volunteer bands my father promptly offered himself, though much against the wish of my mother. His services were at once accepted, and he was given command of a company in the regiment that was formed—principally, I think, because he was an Englishman, and because of the terrible story of the death of his son. This position he very willingly accepted, for the volunteers were chiefly gentlemen, some of whom he had known before. I, too, though hardly thoroughly cured yet, was very eager indeed to offer my services, and though my mother would not allow me to enroll myself as a soldier, she could not refuse me permission to ride along with my father.

With a final chapter to tell you what came of all this, and what happened to us on that expedition into the interior, I shall be able to bring my story to a close.

CHAPTER V

THE REVENGE

THROUGH all that had happened I had never for a moment lost sight of my purpose—of my firm resolve to kill Martinez in revenge for the death of my brother. I had said no word of this either to my father or my mother; I kept it as a kind of pervertedly sacred thing in the recesses of my own mind. I wondered how it would be possible for me to do it, and when a way would open before me; but that some way would open, and that I should do it, I never had the slightest doubt, and when I heard of the formation of that volunteer corps I felt at once that here was my method, and that Providence was pointing out my path. Therefore it was that I immediately resolved to join it, and my mother's refusal to allow me to enroll myself did not trouble me in the least. I fell in with her wishes, of course; but I knew with a deadly certainty that it would nevertheless somehow be managed that I should accompany the column. And when, on starting out, my mother embraced me and adjured me to be careful to avoid all danger, I said to her, with a calm certainty which must have impressed her:

"Mother, you need not fear. I shall come back to you quite safe."

I think I must have believed myself to be an instrument of divine vengeance; I moved through all those stirring scenes like a person in a dream, just as I had endured all through the ten days' march when I was being carried alternately by my father and by Tito, feeling little, caring for nothing, enduring all things, because I was all the time waiting for my day to come, waiting for the moment when my vengeance should leap into active life. A curious state of mind, I know—a very unhealthy state; I am not defending myself; I am merely trying to describe as faithfully as I can exactly what I felt.

In just the same state of mind I rode day after day on my pony, by my father's side, as the troops made their way through the forests in search of the insurgents. The details of those days of marching made no impression upon me; my mental vision was occupied only with one figure, that of Martinez, and regarded him with a steady, ever-burning, never-changing hate. Yet it was not so much even hatred as a calm certainty of doom—the knowledge that I should fulfil my destiny, and that that destiny was to slay this monster.

At last came the day when our guides told us that we were drawing near to the town which Martinez had occupied—that we might hope to come in sight of it by evening. Martinez, however, was ready for us. He had even come out to meet us, and arranged for us an ambush into which we promptly fell. For he had concealed his force in the forest upon our line of route, and they suddenly opened a tremendous fire upon us precisely when we least expected it.

Those Spanish-American troops are never very steady under fire, at the best of times; still less so when that fire comes as a terrifying surprise; and the front of our column wavered and crumpled up under it. Then was shown the advantage of a volunteer troop, whose members, as I have said, were mostly gentlemen by birth. Hearing the firing, and seeing the wavering of the men in front, my father shouted a command to his company, and in a moment we were moving steadily and swiftly forward, the rest of the volunteer regiment following hard on our heels. Instead of dashing into the little glade where the front ranks of our men were being shot down, or whence they were flying in disorder, we promptly scattered out on both sides and rushed through the forest itself upon the hidden soldiers of Martinez, who, thus taken in flank, had to turn and defend themselves.

This charge of the volunteers rallied the regulars, and in a few moments they also were joining in the fray. But that was no organized battle, and rarely had we any opportunity of falling into serried ranks at all. It resolved itself into a series of hand-to-hand combats, fought out among the trees. Friend and foe were so inextricably mingled that it was not always easy to distinguish them, for though the volunteers looked trim enough, many of the Government soldiers were scarcely smarter in appearance than the ragged and ill-appointed free-lances of Martinez.

The rebels fought bravely, for they knew that they were fighting for their lives, as well as for all the fantastic rewards which Martinez had promised them. How far they really believed his stories of the fabulous wealth and power which awaited them, it is difficult to say; it may be that they fully accepted them, for most of them were ignorant enough to believe anything; but at any rate they knew very well that after their capture of the town and the murders that they had committed, no mercy would be shown to any of them who might fall into the hands of the Government. The Government General had hoped to have considerable superiority in numbers. Counting the Indians as well as the mutinous regiments, it is by no means certain that he had any superiority at all.

but it was difficult to form any estimate in a fight that took place in so irregular a manner amidst such unusual surroundings.

There were several open glades in the forest, and twice in the course of that amorphous struggle I took part in a charge, which in each case cleared the glade of the rebels. It is a very curious experience for one who is not used to warfare—to find oneself one of a body of men animated by a single thought, to look at all the faces round one and watch them set in grim determination, fogetting all else but the stern resolve to hurtle down upon the enemy, to trample them underfoot or to drive them away—and to wonder, half-startled, whether one's own face looks like that. Then comes the sharp command, the wild ordered rush onwards, and then the rattle of rifles or the clash of steel, leaping over dead bodies, foe and friend alike, not even noticing which they are, full only of the one idea, to press on, press on. And then the glade is won, and we halt and look back for a moment to see heaps of dead, to see the green grass all trampled and red with blood; and yet there is no time for horror, no time for anything but still that one idea; where are they whom we must conquer? —let us press on, press on.

At least it was so with me. For the earlier part of that fight I kept by my father's side. Quite early my pony was shot and fell under me, but I sprang clear and seized the bridle of a riderless horse as he came past, sprang upon his back (he was far too tall for me) and turned him again into the fray. But in doing this I lost my father for a moment, and could not at once get back to his side. So I ranged through the attle, looking everywhere for the man whom I knew should find. I took my share in the fighting, I suppose; I know that wherever I saw a rebel or an Indian I fired at him, and I think that few of my bullets missed their mark.

But presently my big horse fell, as the pony had done (I think he had been wounded when I first mounted him); and this time I was thrown to the earth with a jar, and it took me a few moments to recover my senses. The rifle which I had carried was injured in the fall; some part of its mechanism was bent, so that when I tried to fire it I could not. I cast it aside, and seized in its stead the nearest weapon that offered, a long naked sword which was lying on the ground in front of me— dropped, I suppose, by some officer as he fell dead, or who perhaps was merely wounded and had crawled aside. I did not stop to think of that; I seized this great sword (far too heavy in reality for me to wield) and started off again on foot, still seeking for what I knew I should find.

By this time the result of the battle was a foregone conclusion. Everywhere the Government troops were steadily driving back the insurgents, and many of the latter were already in flight. It was said afterwards, and I fully believe it, that this success was due to a great extent to the fiery valour of my father. The Colonel in command of the volunteer corps fell, badly wounded, early in the fight, and my father instantly took command and carried the regiment to victory. There were others in it of the same nominal rank as he, yet no one for a moment questioned his assumption of the lead. They think highly over there of the bravery and fighting qualities of the English, and so I suppose it seemed natural to them to follow an Englishman. At any rate they did so, and, civilian though my father was, without any experience in military matters, he led them with dauntless courage, and he led them to victory. If he lacked, as he must have done, knowledge of tactics, that lack mattered comparatively little in this strange hand-to-hand fight in the forest. What told there was personal courage and dash, and of those he had plenty.

I was still far from strong, and I had been racing about for some hours through the battle—and a battle is probably one of the most fatiguing things in the world; yet I had no thought of being tired, no time to feel tired—for no feeling, no thought could be allowed to distract me for an instant from the certainty that God would give my vengeance into my hand. Long I looked for Martinez everywhere, and but for that inner conviction I must have been disappointed. But I knew so surely that I should find him, and that all this vague fighting was a mere preliminary, that I never hesitated for a moment, never doubted for a moment; and at last I saw him.

He stood under a great tree with his back to it, and two of the Government soldiers were attacking him, and for the moment that little group seemed to be apart from all the rest. Perhaps it was only in my mind that they were apart, for I saw that one figure only; and yet I think it is true that there were only the dead for some yards around. The two soldiers were assailing him boldly, and he was defending himself with his sword—the same sword, I thought, with the hatred surging up within me, the same sword that had slain my brother. But he had been famed in earlier days as the best swordsman in the army—some said the best swordsman in South America; and, even while I looked, one of the attacking soldiers went down before him, and then quickly the other, and he stood alone with the light of battle in his eye.

And then—he saw me, as I was springing towards him. His face changed and there came over it a look of diabolical hatred, and yet at the same time, I am sure, a look of fear.

"What", he shouted, "are you here? You have brought all this ill-luck upon me; you and your cursed father and brother!"

"Yes," replied I, "I am here; and I shall kill you."

I sprang straight at him; I might have shot him from a distance, but I meant to kill him with the sword, as he had killed Gerald. I had seen the fear in his eyes—I am sure of that; but now he turned upon me with a laugh of scorn, seeing that I was armed only with a clumsy old sword, and knowing himself a master of his weapon. In a moment we were fencing; I had learnt some fencing at school, yet I doubt whether that was of use to me at this critical moment. I fought by instinct and not by knowledge; yet I must have fought better than I knew, for even as our swords clashed together again and again I saw a change in his eye; I saw the look of triumphant malice fade away and the haunting fear show itself again, I suppose because in some strange unexpected way he could not strike me down at once, because he found me more nearly a match for him than he could possibly have expected.

I think he was scarcely taller than I—I have said that he was a short man; but his reach was longer, and his familiarity with the weapon incomparably greater. My will was indomitable as ever, but my arm was rapidly tiring, and it was only by the most tremendous exertion that I could move that unwieldy sword quickly enough to guard against his lightning-like blows and thrusts. I knew that slowly and surely he was beating down my guard, and that, if he once did that, my fate was sealed. At last, after a shower of mighty blows, came a lightning-like thrust at my heart. I parried, but my failing arm was some infinitesimal fraction of a second later than it should have been. I struck the blade down, but not quite far enough. It was turned from the heart at which it was aimed, but it ran into the fleshy part of my thigh. Springing back after the thrust, as a fencer does, Martinez caught his foot in a root of the tree and went over backwards, his sword falling from his hand. In a moment I leaped upon him, put my foot upon his breast and the point of my sword at his throat. He cried out for mercy.

"Mercy!" I said, jerkily perhaps, for I was panting from the terrible exertion of the fight; "what mercy did you show to my brother?"

And I pressed the point of the sword upon his throat.

Yet again he shrieked for mercy. Somehow in some previous part of the struggle the breast of my shirt had been torn open, and the little silver and ebony crucifix which my mother had fastened round my neck was hanging outwards as I stooped over him.

"Mercy!" he said, "for the sake of the Christ whose image you wear!"

A half laugh came from me to hear this renegade, who had tried to make me trample on the crucifix, now begging for his life in the name of that same Christ whose image he had profaned. But not for that would I be turned aside.

I had recovered my breath by now, and I drew back my arm to make the final thrust, when suddenly that arm was stayed. Once more beside me stood my brother, looking up earnestly into my face, and holding back with his little hand the arm that would have avenged him. This time at least it was no hallucination, for Martinez saw it too. I saw the awful look of terror in his eyes; I saw the sweat of fear break out upon his face as he groaned in horror. But I looked into the eyes of the dead. My brother's hand was on my arm, and he was looking up gravely, earnestly, pleadingly, into my face. I could not kill his murderer now. As I threw down my sword and drew back with a strange emptiness in my heart, the most lovely and loving smile broke out over my brother's face, and then once more he was gone. As I turned away from the prostrate Martinez, he drew a knife out of the leg of his long leather boot, and stabbed at me even as I was retiring. I sprang aside instinctively, and before he could rise to his feet a little knot of the Government soldiers came racing up and sprang upon him, wrested his knife from him and made him their prisoner.

Still with that strange empty feeling I turned on my heel, and was about to go I know not where, when I caught sight of the forbidding face of Antinahuel taking aim at me with a rifle over the top of a bush. My movement was more instinctive than reasoned; with the quickness of long practice I drew out the revolver from my belt, and two reports sounded together. I felt a numbing blow in my right arm, and the pistol fell from it, to the ground; but before I myself sank down beside it I had time to note the horrible blue hole in Antinahuel's forehead—blue for a moment, before the blood gushed out of it as he fell backwards. I myself fell also, for the blood was pouring from the wound in my thigh, in addition to the shock caused by the rifle bullet; and so for a time all knowledge of mundane affairs passed from me.

When I came to myself again it was dark night, and I lay for a time watching the stars, still hardly conscious, hardly able to think of my present situation and caring nothing for the future, conscious chiefly of one thing—an awful thirst produced no doubt by the great drain of blood from the body. I had suffered much at many periods of my story, as you know by this time; yet I think that nothing that I suffered was ever so terrible as that thirst while I lay helpless under the stars. The night seemed to be years in length; sometimes I seemed to be unconscious for a few moments, and then I woke with the conviction that I must have slept through a day, and that another night had come upon me, and yet when I looked at the stars I saw that they had scarcely moved.

I lost all count of time, but somewhere amid what seemed the centuries I realized uncertainly that some lanterns were approaching, and presently with a start of joy I heard my father's voice, and saw his face bending over me. I cried to him for water, and in a moment he held a flask to my lips, and then I think I must have swooned again for pure joy that that thirst was allayed. Quickly now my wounds were bandaged and I was carried gently away from the field.

And here to all intents and purposes my story ends. Of what avail to tell of my slow nursing back to health and strength, of the thanks given both to my father and to me by the Government of the country, and the decorations it bestowed upon us for the victory which, it said in its politeness, was so largely due to our bravery? What need I say of that day a month later, when I stood silently watching amidst a mob howling out execrations, while Martinez was shot in the great square of the capital? The hatred had gone—gone utterly out of my life, wiped out of it by the touch of the dead. No, not of the dead, but of the living, for I had looked into my brother's eyes, and I knew that he lived and loved me still. And so I was content, though then I knew nothing of the beautiful fate which would bring my brother back to life fifteen years later in a country far away, which would bring him in that new body into my life again, which would enable us both to recognize one another, and to realize that death can never part those souls that truly love.

Other books by Charles W. Leadbeater

The Astral Plane
A clairvoyant describes life after death.

The Chakras
A description of the psychic force centers in man's body. With 10 color paintings.

Clairvoyance
A first hand account of what extra-sensory-perception is all about.

The Inner Life
Detailed, in depth description of man's unseen nature and the universe.

Life After Death
What's it like to die? Based upon the theosophical philosophy.

Man, Visible and Invisible
The colors in man's aura. Includes 26 illustrations.

The Masters and the Path
The personalities, home life, work, nature, powers of the Mahatmas.

Thought Forms (with Annie Besant)
What do our thoughts look like? With 58 colored and black and white illustrations.

These titles are available from:
QUEST BOOKS
306 West Geneva Road
Wheaton, Illinois 60187